SCOTLAND'S MARK ON AMERICA

By

GEORGE FRASER BLACK, Ph.D.

With a Foreword

By JOHN FOORD

Published by
The Scottish Section of "America's Making"
New York, 1921

251464

FOREWORD

It has been said that the Scot is never so much at home as when he is abroad. Under this half-jesting reference to one of the characteristics of our race, there abides a sober truth, namely, that the Scotsman carries with him from his parent home into the world without no half-hearted acceptance of the duties required of him in the land of his adoption. He is usually a public-spirited citizen, a useful member of society, wherever you find him. But that does not lessen the warmth of his attachment to the place of his birth, or the land of his forbears. Be his connection with Scotland near or remote, there is enshrined in the inner sanctuary of his heart, memories, sentiments, yearnings, that are the heritage of generations with whom love of their country was a dominant passion, and pride in the deeds that her children have done an incentive to effort and an antidote against all that was base or ignoble.

It is a fact that goes to the core of the secular struggle for human freedom that whole-hearted Americanism finds no jarring note in the sentiment of the Scot, be that sentiment ever so intense. In the sedulous cultivation of the Scottish spirit there is nothing alien, and, still more emphatically, nothing harmful, to the institutions under which we live. The things that nourish the one, engender attachment and loyalty to the other. So, as we cherish the memories of the Motherland, keep in touch with the simple annals of our childhood's home, or the home of our kin, bask in the fireside glow of its homely humor, or dwell in imagination amid the haunts of old romance, we are tne better Americans for the Scottish heritage from which heart and mind alike derive inspiration and delight.

‣ It is as difficult to separate the current of Scottish migration to the American Colonies, or to the United States that grew out of them, from the larger stream which issued from England, as it is to distinguish during the last two hundred years the contributions by Scotsmen from those of Englishmen to the great body of English literature. We have the first census of the new Republic, in the year 1790, and an investigator who classified this enumeration according to what he conceived to be the nationality of the names, found that the total free, white, population numbering 3,250,000 contained 2,345,844 people of English origin; 188,589 of Scottish origin, and 44,273 of Irish origin.

3

The system of classification is manifestly loose, and the distribution of
parent nationalities entirely at variance with known facts. That part
of the population described as Irish was largely Ulster-Scottish, the
true Irish never having emigrated in any considerable numbers until
they felt the pressure of the potato famine, fifty years later. There is
excellent authority for the statement that, at the outbreak of the
Revolutionary War one-third of the entire population of Pennsylvania was of Ulster-Scottish origin. A New England historian,
quoted by Whitelaw Reid, counts that between 1730 and 1770 at least
half a million souls were transferred from Ulster to the Colonies—
more than half of the Presbyterian population of Ulster—and that
at the time of the Revolution they made one-sixth of the total population of the nascent Republic. Another authority fixes the inhabitants
of Scottish ancestry in the nine Colonies south of New England at
about 385,000. He counts that less than half of the entire population
of the Colonies was of English origin, and that nearly, or quite one-
third of it, had a direct Scottish ancestry.

These conclusions find powerful support in the number of distinguished men whom the Scots and the Ulstermen contributed to the
Revolutionary struggle, and to the public life of the early days of the
United States. Out of Washington's twenty-two brigadier generals,
nine were of Scottish descent, and one of the greatest achievements
of the war—the rescue of Kentucky and the whole rich territory
northwest of the Ohio, from which five States were formed—was that
of General George Rogers Clark, a Scottish native of Albert County,
Virginia. When the Supreme Court of the United States was first
organized by Washington three of the four Associate Justices were of
the same blood—one a Scot and two Ulster-Scots. When the first
Chief Justice, John Jay, left the bench, his successor, John Rutledge,
was an Ulster-Scot. Washington's first cabinet contained four members—two of them were Scotch and the third was an Ulster-Scot.
Out of the fifty-six members who composed the Congress that adopted
the Declaration of Independence eleven were of Scottish descent. It
was in response to the appeal of a Scot, John Witherspoon, that the
Declaration was signed; it is preserved in the handwriting of an
Ulster-Scot who was Secretary of the Congress; it was first publicly
read to the people by an Ulster-Scot, and first printed by a third
member of the same vigorous body of early settlers.

George Bancroft will hardly be accused of holding a brief for the
Scot in American history but, with all his New England predi'·ctions,
he frankly records this conclusion: "We shall find the first voice publicly raised in America to dissolve all connection with Great Britain,
came not from the Puritans of New England, or the Dutch of New

York, or the planters of Virginia, but from Scotch-Irish Presbyterians." It was Patrick Henry, a Scot, who kindled the popular flame for independence. The foremost, the most irreconcilable, the most determined in pushing the quarrel to the last extremity, were those whom the bishops and Lord Donegal & Company had been pleased to drive out of Ulster.

The distinguished place which men of Scottish or of Ulster origin had asserted for themselves in the councils of the Colonies was not lost when the Colonies became independent States. Among the first of the thirteen original States two-thirds were of either Scottish or Ulster-Scottish origin. Of the men who have filled the great office of President of the United States, eleven out of the whole twenty-five come under the same category. About half the Secretaries of the Treasury of the Government of the United States have been of Scottish descent, and nearly a third of the Secretaries of State.

But it is perhaps in the intangible things that go to the making of national character that the Scottish contribution to the making of America has been most notable. In 1801, the population of the whole of Scotland was but little over a million and a half, and behind that there were at least eight centuries of national history. Behind that, too, were all the long generations of toil and strife in which the Scottish character was being molded into the forms that Scott and Burns made immortal. It is a character full of curious contrasts, with its strong predilection for theology and metaphysics on one side, and for poetry and romance on the other. Hard, dry and practical in its attitude to the ordinary affairs of life, it is apt to catch fire from a sudden enthusiasm, as if volatility were its dominant note and instability its only fixed attribute. And so it has come about that side by side with tomes of Calvinistic divinity, there has been transmitted to Scotsmen an equally characteristic product of the mind of their race— a body of folksong, of ballad poetry, of legend and of story in that quaint and copious Doric speech which makes so direct an appeal to the hearts of men whether they are to the manner born or not. It is surely a paradox that a nation which, in the making, had the hardest kind of work to extract a scanty living from a stubborn soil, and still harder work to defend their independence, their liberties, their faith from foes of their own kindred, should be best known to the world for the romantic ideals they have cherished and the chivalrous follies for which their blood has been shed.

But, it is well to remember that long before the Reformers of the sixteenth century founded the parish school system of Scotland, the monasteries had their schools and so had the parish churches; there were high schools in the burghs and song schools of remarkable excellence. The light of learning may have waxed dim at times, but it was not from an illiterate land that Scottish scholars carried into Europe all through the Middle Ages the name and fame of 'heir country, any more than it was from a people unversed in the arts of war that Scottish soldiers went abroad to fight foreign battles, giving now a Constable to France, a General-in-Chief to Russia and still again a Lieutenant to Gustavus Adolphus. If evidence were needed of the vigor of the Scottish race, it is readily forthcoming in the fact that for five hundred years the Land O'Cakes enriched the world with the surplus of her able men.

Nurse of heroes, nurse of martyrs, nurse of freemen, are titles which belong of right to our Motherland and she has been justified of her children, at home and abroad. The rolls of honor of many countries and many climes bear their names; there is no field of distinction whether it be of thought or of action that has not witnessed their triumphs. That Scotland has yielded more than her share of the men who have gone forth to the conquest of the world is largely due to the fact that it was part of her discipline that men must first conquer themselves. The weakest of them felt that restraining influence, and the striving after the Scottish ideal, however feeble, has been a protection against sinking into utter baseness. The most wayward scions of the Scottish family have known that influence, and have borne testimony to the beauty of the homely virtues which they falied to practice and the nobility of aspirations which fell short of controlling their life.

It belongs to the character and antecedents of Scotsmen that the attribute of national independence should take so high a place among the objects of human effort and desire. It was because Scotland settled for all time, six hundred years ago, her place as an independent State that she proved herself capable of begetting men like John Knox, Robert Burns and Walter Scott. It is because the vigor of the Scottish race and the adaptiveness of the Scottish genius remain today unimpaired, that the lustre of Scottish names shone so brilliantly during the World War. It may be confidently asserted that, whether regarded as a race or a people no members of the great English-speaking family did more promptly, more cheerfully or more courageously make the sacrifices required to perform their full part in the struggle to defend the freedom that belongs to our common heritage and to preserve the ideals without which we should not regard life as worth living. The union, centuries old, in the Scottish mind and heart of the most uncompromising devotion to individual liberty with the most fervid patriotism, is a sentiment of which the world stands greatly in need today. We need not go far to find evi-

dence of how perilous it is to sink regard for the great conception
of human brotherhood in a narrow, nationalistic concern for individual interests.   In the Scottish conception of liberty, *duties* have
always been rated as highly as *rights;* it has been a constructive, not
a destructive formula; it has been an inspiration to raise men out of
themselves, not to prompt them to indulge in antics of promiscuous
leveling.   The kind of democracy for which Scotsmen have deemed
that the world should be made safe is a human brotherhood, indeed,
but a brotherhood imbued with the generous rivalry of effort, the
enthusiasm of emulous achievement, and not one of inglorious,
monotonous and colorless equality.   JOHN FOORD

CONTENTS

"No people so few in number have scored so deep a mark in the world's history as the Scots have done. No people have a greater right to be proud of their blood."—*James Anthony Froude.*

Scotland's Mark on America

SCOTTISH EMIGRATION TO THE AMERICAN COLONIES

Scottish emigration to America came in two streams—one direct from the motherland and the other through the province of Ulster in the north of Ireland. Those who came by this second route are usually known as "Ulster Scots," or more commonly as "Scotch-Irish," and they have been claimed as Irishmen by Irish writers in the United States. This is perhaps excusable but hardly just. Throughout their residence in Ireland the Scots settlers preserved their distinctive Scottish characteristics, and generally described themselves as "the Scottish nation in the north of Ireland." They, of course, like the early pioneers in this country, experienced certain changes through the influence of their new surroundings, but, as one writer has remarked, they "remained as distinct from the native population as if they had never crossed the Channel. They were among the Irish but not of them." Their sons, too, when they attended the classes in the University of Glasgow, signed the matriculation register as "A Scot of Ireland." They did not intermarry with the native Irish, though they did intermarry to some extent with the English Puritans and with the French Huguenots. (These Huguenots were colonies driven out of France by the Revocation of the Edict of Nantes in 1685, and induced to settle in the north of Ireland by William III. To this people Ireland is indebted for its lace industry, which they introduced into that country.)

Again many Irish-American writers on the Scots Plantation of Ulster have assumed that the Scots settlers were entirely or almost of Gaelic origin, ignoring the fact, if they were aware of it, that the people of the Scottish lowlands were "almost as English in racial derivation as if they had come from the North of England." Parker, the historian of Londonderry, New Hampshire, speaking of the early Scots settlers in New England, has well said: "Although they came to this land from Ireland, where their ancestors had a century before planted themselves, yet they retained unmixed the national Scotch character.

11

Nothing sooner offended them than to be called Irish. Their antipathy to this appellation had its origin in the hostility then existing in Ireland between the Celtic race, the native Irish, and the English and Scotch colonists." Belknap, in his *History of New Hampshire* (Boston, 1791) quotes a letter from the Rev. James MacGregor (1677-1729) to Governor Shute in which the writer says: "We are surprised to hear ourselves termed Irish people, when we so frequently ventured our all for the British Crown and liberties against the Irish papists, and gave all tests of our loyalty, which the government of Ireland required, and are always ready to do the same when demanded."

Down to the present day the descendants of these Ulster Scots settlers living in the United States who have maintained an interest in their origin, always insist that they are of Scottish and not of Irish origin. On this point it will be sufficient to quote the late Hon. Leonard Allison Morrison, of New Hampshire. Writing twenty-five years ago he said: "I am one of Scotch-Irish blood and my ancestor came with Rev. McGregor of Londonderry, and neither he nor any of their descendants were willing to be called 'merely Irish.' I have twice visited," he adds, "the parish of Aghadowney, Co. Londonderry, from which they came, in Ireland, and all that locality is filled, not with 'Irish' but with Scotch-Irish, and this is pure Scotch blood today, after more than 200 years." The mountaineers of Tennessee and Kentucky are largely the descendants of these same Ulster Scots, and their origin is conclusively shown by the phrase used by mothers to their unruly children: "If you don't behave, Clavers [i. e., Claverhouse] will get you."

If we must continue to use the hyphen when referring to these early immigrants it is preferable to use the term "Ulster Scot" instead of "Scotch-Irish," as was pointed out by the late Whitelaw Reid, because it does not confuse the race with the accident of birth, and because the people preferred it themselves. "If these Scottish and Presbyterian colonists," he says, "must be called Irish because they had been one or two generations in the north of Ireland, then the Pilgrim Fathers, who had been one generation or more in Holland, must by the same reasoning be called Dutch or at the very least English Dutch."

To understand the reasons for the Scots colonization of Ulster and the replantation in America it is necessary to look back three centuries in British history. On the crushing of the Irish rebellion under Sir Cahir O'Dogherty in 1607 about 500,000 acres of forfeited land in the province of Ulster were at the disposal of the crown. At the suggestion of King James the I. of England, Ulster was divided into lots and offered to colonists from England. Circumstances, however, turned what was mainly intended to be an English enterprise into a Scottish one. Scottish participation "which does not seem to have been originally regarded as important," became eventually, as Ford points out, the mainstay of the enterprise. "Although from the first there was an understanding between [Sir Arthur] Chichester and the English Privy Council that eventually the plantation would be opened to Scotch settlers, no steps were taken in that direction until the plan had been matured . . . The first public announcement of any Scottish connection with the Ulster plantation appears in a letter of March 19, 1609, from Sir Alexander Hay, the Scottish secretary resident at the English Court, to the Scottish Privy Council at Edinburgh." In this communication Hay announced that the king "out of his unspeikable love and tindir affectioun" for his Scottish subjects had decided that they were to be allowed a share, and he adds, that here is a great opportunity for Scotland since "we haif greitt advantaige of transporting of our men and bestiall [i. e., live stock of a farm] in regairde we lye so neir to that coiste of Ulster." Immediately on receipt of this letter the Scottish Privy Council made public proclamation of the news and announced that those of them "quho ar disposit to tak ony land in Yreland" were to present their desires and petitions to the Council. The first application enrolled was by "James Andirsoun portionair of Litle Govane," and by the 14th of September seventy-seven Scots had come forward as purchasers. If their offers had been accepted, they would have possessed among them 141,000 acres of land. In 1611, in consequence of a rearrangement of applicants the number of favored Scots was reduced to fifty-nine, with eighty-one thousand acres of land at their disposal. Each of these "Undertakers," as they were called, was accompanied to his new home by kinsmen, friends, and tenants, as Lord Ochiltree, for instance, who is mentioned as having arrived "accompanied with thirty-three followers, a minister, some tenants, freeholders, [and] artificers." By the end of 1612 the emigration from Scotland is estimated to have reached 10,000. Indeed, before the end of this year so rapidly had the traffic increased between Scotland and Ireland that the passage between the southwest of Scotland and Ulster "is now become a commoun and ane ordinarie ferrie," the boatmen of which were having a rare time of it by charging what they pleased for the passage or freight. In the selection of the settlers measures were carefully taken that they should be "from the inwards part of Scotland," and that they should be so located in Ulster that "they may not mix nor inter-marry" with "the mere Irish." For the most part the settlers appear to have been selected from the shires of Dumbarton, Renfrew, Ayr, Galloway, and Dumfries. Emigration from Scotland to Ireland appears to have continued steadily and the

English historian Carte estimated, after diligent documentary study, that by 1641 there were in Ulster 100,000 Scots and 20,000 English settlers. In 1656 it was proposed by the Irish government that persons "of the Scottish nation desiring to come into Ireland" should be prohibited from settling in Ulster or County Louth, but the scheme was not put into effect. Governmental opposition notwithstanding emigration from Scotland to Ireland appears to have continued steadily, and after the Revolution of 1688 there seems to have been a further increase. Archbishop Synge estimated that by 1715 not less than 50,000 Scottish families had settled in Ulster during these twenty-seven years. It should be also mentioned that "before the Ulster plantation began there was already a considerable Scottish occupation of the region nearest to Scotland. These Scottish settlements were confined to counties Down and Antrim, which were not included in the scheme of the plantation. Their existence facilitated Scottish emigration to the plantation and they were influential in giving the plantation the Scottish character which it promptly acquired. Although planned to be in the main an English settlement, with one whole county turned over to the city of London alone, it soon became in the main a Scottish settlement."

The Scots were not long settled in Ulster before misfortune and persecution began to harass them. The Irish rebellion of 1641, said by some to have been an outbreak directed against the Scottish and English settlers, regarded by the native Irish as intruders and usurpers, caused them much suffering; and Harrison says that for "several years afterward 12,000 emigrants annually left Ulster for the American plantations." The Revolution of 1688 was also long and bloody in Ireland and the sufferings of the settlers reached a climax in the siege of Londonderry (April to August, 1688). They suffered also from the restrictions laid upon their industries and commerce by the English government. These restrictions, and later the falling in of leases, rack-renting by the landlords, payment of tithes for support of a church with which they had no connection, and several other burdens and annoyances, were the motives which impelled emigration to the American colonies from 1718 onwards. Five ships bearing seven hundred Ulster Scots emigrants arrived in Boston on August 4, 1718, under the leadership of Rev. William Boyd. They were allowed to select a township site of twelve miles square at any place on the frontiers. A few settled at Portland, Maine, at Wicasset, and at Worcester and Haverhill, Massachusetts, but the greater number finally at Londonderry, New Hampshire. In 1723-4 they built a parsonage and a church for their minister, Rev. James MacGregor. In six years they had four schools, and within nine years Londonderry paid one-fifteenth of the state tax. Previous to the Revolution of 1776 ten distinct settlements were made by colonists from Londonderry, N. H., all of which became towns of influence and importance. Notable among the descendants of these colonists were Matthew Thornton, Henry Knox, Gen. John Stark, Hugh McCulloch, Horace Greeley, Gen. George B. McClellan, Salmon P. Chase, and Asa Gray. From 1771 to 1773 "the whole emigration from Ulster is estimated at 30,000 of whom 10,000 were weavers."

In 1706 the Rev. Cotton Mather put forth a plan to settle hardy Scots families on the frontiers of Maine and New Hampshire to protect the towns and churches there from the French and Indians, the Puritans evidently not being able to protect themselves. He says, "I write letters unto diverse persons of Honour both in Scotland and in England; to procure Settlements of Good Scotch Colonies, to the Northward of us. This may be a thing of great consequence;" and elsewhere he suggests that a Scottish colony might be of good service in getting possession of Nova Scotia. In 1735, twenty-seven families, and in 1753 a company of sixty adults and a number of children, collected in Scotland by General Samuel Waldo, were landed at George's River, Maine. In honor of the ancient capital of their native country, they named their settlement Stirling.

Another and an important cause of the early appearance of Scots in America was the wars between Scotland and England during the Commonwealth. Large numbers of Scottish prisoners taken at Dunbar (1650) and at Worcester (1651) were sold into service in the colonies, a shipload arriving in Boston Harbor in 1652 on the ship *John and Sara*. The means taken to ameliorate their condition led in 1657 to the foundation of the Scots Charitable Society of Boston—the earliest known Scottish society in America. Its foundation may be taken as evidence that there were already prosperous and influential Scots living in Boston at that time. A list of the passengers of the *John and Sara* is given in Suffolk *Deed Records* (bk. 1, pp. 5-6) and in Drake's *The Founders of New England* (Boston, 1860, pp. 74-76). These men, says Boulton, "worked out their terms of servitude at the Lynn iron works and elsewhere, and founded honorable families whose Scotch names appear upon our early records. No account exists of the Scotch prisoners that were sent to New England in Cromwell's time; at York in 1650 were the Maxwells, McIntires, and Grants. The Mackclothlans' [i. e., Mac Lachlans], later known as the Claflins, gave a governor to Massachusetts and distinguished merchants to New York City."

The bitter persecution of Presbyterians during the periods of episcopal rule in the latter half of the seventeenth century also contributed

largely to Scottish emigration to the new world.   A Scottish merchant
in Boston named Hugh Campbell, obtained permission from the
authorities of the Bay State Colony in February 1679-80 to bring in a
number of settlers from Scotland and to establish them in the Nepmug
country in the vicinity of Springfield, Massachusetts.

So desperate had matters become in Scotland at the beginning of
the eighth decade of the seventeenth century that a number of the
nobility and gentry determined to settle in New Jersey and the Caro-
linas.   One of these colonies was founded in New Jersey in 1682 under
the management of James Drummond, Earl of Perth, John Drummond, Robert Barclay the Quaker Apologist. David and John Barclay, his brothers, Robert Gordon, Gawen Lawrie, and George Wil-
locks.   In 1684 Gawen Lawrie, who had been for several years previously residing in the colony, was appointed Deputy Governor of the
province and fixed his residence at Elizabeth.   In the same year Perth
(so named in honor of the Earl of Perth, one of the principal proprietors, now Perth Amboy) was made the capital of the new Scottish
settlement.   During the following century a constant stream of emigrants both from Scotland and from Ulster came to the colony.   One
of the principal encouragers of the Scottish colony in New Jersey
was George Scot or Scott (d. 1685) of Pitlochrie, who had been repeatedly fined and imprisoned by the Privy Council of Scotland for
attending "Conventicles," as clandestine religious gatherings were then
called in Scotland, and in the hope of obtaining freedom of worship
in the new world he proposed to emigrate "to the plantations."   To
encourage others to do the like he printed at Edinburgh (1685) a work,
now very rare, called "The Model of the Government of the Province
of East New Jersey, in America; and Encouragement for Such as
Design to be concerned there."   Scot received a grant of five hundred
acres in recognition of his having written the work, and sailed in the
Henry and Francis for America.   A malignant fever broke out among
the passengers and nearly half on board perished including Scot and
his wife. A son and daughter survived and the proprietors a year after
issued a confirmation of the grant to Scot's daughter and her husband
(John Johnstone); many of whose descendants are still living in New
Jersey.

Walter Ker of Dalserf, Lanarkshire, banished in 1685, settled in
Freehold, and was active in organizing the Presbyterian Church there,
one of the oldest in New Jersey.   The Scots settlers who came over
at this period occupied most of the northern counties of the state but
many went south and southwest, mainly around Princeton, and, says
Samuel Smith, the first historian of the province, "There were very
soon four towns in the Province, viz., Elizabeth, Newark, Middletown

and Shrewsbury; and these with the country round were in a few years plentifully inhabited by the accession of the Scotch, of whom there came a great many." These Scots, says Duncan Campbell, largely gave "character to this sturdy little state not the least of their achievements being the building up if not the nominal founding of Princeton College, which has contributed so largely to the scholarship of America."

In 1682 another company of nobles and gentlemen in Scotland arranged for a settlement at Port Royal, South Carolina. These colonists consisted mainly of Presbyterians banished for attending "Conventicles." The names of some of these immigrants, whose descendants exist in great numbers at the present day, included James McClintock, John Buchanan, William Inglis, Gavin Black, Adam Allan, John Galt, Thomas Marshall, William Smith, Robert Urie, Thomas Bryce, John Syme, John Alexander, John Marshall, Matthew Machen, John Paton, John Gibson, John Young, Arthur Cunningham, George Smith, and George Dowart. The colony was further increased by a small remnant of the ill-fated expedition to Darien. One of the vessels which left Darien to return to Scotland, the *Rising Sun*, was driven out of its course by a gale and took refuge in Charleston. Among its passengers was the Rev. Archibald Stobo, who was asked by some people in Charleston to preach in the town while the ship was being refitted. He accepted the invitation and left the ship with his wife and about a dozen others. The following day, the *Rising Sun*, while lying off the bar, was overwhelmed in a hurricane and all on board were drowned. This Rev. Archibald Stobo was the earliest American ancestor of the late Theodore Roosevelt's mother. In the following year (1683) the colony was augmented by a number of Scots colonists from Ulster led by one Ferguson. A second Scottish colony in the same year under Henry Erskine, Lord Cardross, founded Stuartstown (so named in honor of his wife). Another colony from Ulster was that of Williamsburgh township (1732-34), who named their principal village Kingstree.

There were settlements of Scots Highlanders in North Carolina, on the Cape Fear River, as early as 1729; some indeed are said to have settled there as early as 1715. Neill McNeill of Jura brought over a colony of more than 350 from Argyllshire in 1739, and large numbers in 1746, after Culloden, and settled them on the Cape Fear River. Cross Creek, now Fayetteville, was the center of these Highland settlements, and hither came the Scottish heroine, Flora MacDonald, in 1775. The mania for emigration to North Carolina affected all classes in Scotland and continued for many years. The *Scots Magazine* for May 1768 records that a number of settlers from the

Western Isles had embarked for Carolina and Georgia, including forty or fifty families from Jura alone. In September of following year it is stated that a hundred families of Highlanders had arrived at Brunswick, North Carolina, and "two vessels are daily expected with more." In August 1769 the ship *Mally* sailed from Islay full of passengers for North Carolina, which was the third or fourth emigration from Argyll "since the conclusion of the late war." In August 1770 it was stated that since the previous April six vessels carrying about twelve hundred emigrants had sailed from the western Highlands for North Carolina. In February of the following year the same magazine states that five hundred souls in Islay and adjacent islands were preparing to emigrate to America in the following summer. In September of the same year three hundred and seventy persons sailed from Skye for North Carolina, and two entries in the magazine for 1772 record the emigration of numbers from Sutherland and Loch Erribol. In the same year a writer says the people who have emigrated from the Western Isles since the year 1768 "have carried with them at least ten thousand pounds in specie. Notwithstanding this is a great loss to us, yet the depopulation by these emigrations is a much greater. . . . Besides, the continual emigrations from Ireland and Scotland, will soon render our colonies independent on the mother-country." In August, 1773, three gentlemen of the name of Macdonell, with their families and four hundred Highlanders from Inverness-shire sailed for America to take possession of a grant of land "in Albany." On the 22d of June previously between seven and eight hundred peopl. from the Lewis sailed from Stornoway for the colonies. On the first of September, 1773, four hundred and twenty-five men, women and children from Inverness-shire sailed for America. "They are the finest set of fellows in the Highlands. It is allowed they carried at least 6000 pounds Sterling in ready cash with them." In 1774 farmers and heads of families in Stirlingshire were forming societies to emigrate to the colonies and the fever had also extended to Orkney and Shetland and the north of England. In 1753 it was estimated that there were one thousand Scots in the single county of Cumberland capable of bearing arms, of whom the Macdonalds were the most numerous. Gabriel Johnston, governor of the province of North Carolina from 1734 to 1752, appears to have done more to encourage the settlement of Scots in the colony than all its other colonial governors combined.

In 1735 a body of one hundred and thirty Highlanders with fifty women and children sailed from Inverness and landed at Savannah in January 1736. They were under the leadership of Lieutenant Hugh Mackay. Some Carolinians endeavoured to dissuade them from going to the South by telling them that the Spaniards would attack them from their houses in the fort near where they were to settle, to which they replied, "Why, then, we will beat them out of their fort, and shall have houses ready built to live in." "This valiant spirit," says Jones, "found subsequent expression in the efficient military service rendered by these Highlanders during the wars between the Colonists and the Spaniards, and by their descendants in the American Revolution. To John 'More' McIntosh, Captain Hugh Mackay, Ensign Charles Mackay, Col. John McIntosh, General Lachlan McIntosh, and their gallant comrades and followers, Georgia, both as a Colony and a State, owes a large debt of gratitude. This settlement was subsequently augmented from time to time by fresh arrivals from Scotland. . . . Its men were prompt and efficient in arms, and when the war cloud descended upon the southern confines of the province no defenders were more alert or capable than those found in the ranks of these Highlanders." "No people," says Walter Glasco Charlton, "ever came to Georgia who took so quickly to the conditions under which they were to live or remained more loyal to her interests" than the Highlanders. "These men," says Jones, "were not reckless adventurers or reduced emigrants volunteering through necessity, or exiled through insolvency or want. They were men of good character, and were carefully selected for their military qualities. . . . Besides this military band, others among the Mackays, the Dunbars, the Baillies, and the Cuthberts applied for large tracts of land in Georgia which they occupied with their own servants. Many of them went over in person and settled in the province."

Among the immigrants who flocked into Virginia in 1729 and 1740 we find individuals named Alexander Breckinridge, David Logan, Hugh Campbell, William Graham, Jámes Waddell (the "Blind Preacher"), John McCue, Benjamin Erwin, Gideon Blackburn, Samuel Houston, Archibald Scott, Samuel Carrack, John Montgomery, George Baxter, William McPheeters, and Robert Poage (Page?), and others bearing the names of Bell, Trimble (Turnbull), Hay, Anderson, Patterson, Scott, Wilson, and Young. John McDowell and eight of his men were killed by Indians in 1742. Among the members of his company was his venerable father Ephraim McDowell. In 1763 the Indians attacked a peaceful settlement and carried off a number of captives. After traveling some distance and feeling safe from pursuit they demanded that their captives should sing for their entertainment, and it was a Scotswoman, Mrs. Gilmore, who struck up Rouse's version of the one hundred and thirty-seventh psalm:

"By Babel's streams we sat and wept,
    When Zion we thought on,
In midst thereof we hanged our harps
    The willow tree thereon.

"For there a song required they,
    Who did us captive bring;
Our spoilers called for mirth, and said:
    'A song of Zion sing.' "

In the following year Colonel Henry Bouquet led a strong force against the Indians west of the Ohio, and compelled them to desist from their predatory warfare, and deliver up the captives they had taken. One of his companies was made up of men from the Central Valley of Virginia, largely composed of Scots or men of Ulster Scot descent, and commanded by Alexander McClanahan, a good Galloway surname. Ten years later occurred the battle of Point Pleasant when men of the same race under the command of Andrew Lewis defeated the Shawnee Indians.

In January 1775, the freeholders of Fincastle presented an address to the Continental Congress, declaring their purpose to resist the oppressive measures of the home government. Among the signers were William Christian, Rev. Charles Cummings, Arthur Campbell, William Campbell, William Edmundson, William Preston and others. Several other counties in the same state, inhabited mainly by Scots or people of Scottish descent, adopted like resolutions. During the Revolutionary war, in addition to large numbers of men of Scottish origin serving in the Continental army from this state, the militia were also constantly in service under the leadership of such men as Colonels Samuel McDowell, George Moffett, William Preston, John and William Bowyer, Samson Mathews, etc.

The following Scots were members of His Majesty's Council in South Carolina under the royal government, from 1720 to 1776: Alexander Skene, James Kinloch (1729), John Cleland, James Graeme, George Saxby, James Michie, John Rattray (1761), Thomas Knox Gordon, and John Stuart. Andrew Rutledge was Speaker of the Commons' House of Assembly from 1749 to 1752. David Graeme, attorney at law in 1754, was Attorney-General of the State from 1757 to 1764. James Graeme, most probably a relation of the preceding, was elected to the Assembly from Port Royal in 1732, became Judge of the Court of Vice Admiralty from 1742 to 1752, and Chief Justice from 1749 to 1752. James Michie was Speaker of the Assembly from 1752 to 1754, Judge of the Court of Admiralty from 1752 to 1754, and Chief Justice from 1759 to 1761. William Simpson served as Chief Justice 1761-1762. Thomas Knox Gordon was appointed Chief Justice in 1771 and served till 1776, and in 1773 he also appears as Member of Council. John Murray was appointed. Associate Justice in 1771 and died in 1774. William Gregory was appointed by His Majesty's mandamus to succeed him in 1774. Robert Hume was Speaker of the Assembly in 1732-1733. Robert Brisbane was Associate Justice in 1764, and Robert Pringle appears in the same office in 1760 and 1766. John Rattray was Judge of the Court of Vice-Admiralty in 1760-61, and James Abercrombie appears as Attorney-General in 1731-32. James Simpson was Clerk of the Council in 1773, Surveyor-General of Land in 1772, Attorney-General in 1774-75, and Judge of Vice-Admiralty in the absence of Sir Augustus Johnson in 1769. John Carwood was Assistant Justice in 1725. Thomas Nairne was employed in 1707 "as resident agent among the Indians, with power to settle all disputes among traders . . . to arrest traders who were guilty of misdemeanors and send them to Charleston for trial, to take charge of the goods of persons who were committed to prison, and to exercise the power of a justice of the peace." This Thomas Nairne is probably the same individual who published, anonymously, "A letter from South Carolina; giving an account of the soil . . . product . . . trade . . . government [etc.] of that province. Written by a Swiss Gentleman to his friend at Bern," the first edition of which was published in London in 1710 (second ed. in 1732).

Among the names of the seventeen corporate members of the Charleston Library Society established in 1743 occur those of the following Scots: Robert Brisbane, Alexander M'Cauley, Patrick M'Kie, William Logan, John Sinclair, James Grindlay, Alexander Baron, and Charles Stevenson.

Of the members of the Provincial Congress held at Charleston in January, 1775, the following were Scotsmen or men of Scottish ancestry: Major John Caldwell, Patrick Calhoun (ancestor of Vice-President Calhoun), George Haig of the family of Bemersyde, Charles Elliott, Thomas Ferguson, Adam Macdonald, Alexander M'Intosh, John M'Ness, Isaac MacPherson, Col. William Moultrie, David Oliphant, George Ross, Thomas Rutledge, James Sinkler, James Skirving, senior, James Skirving, junior, William Skirving, and Rev. William Tennent.

In Maryland there seems to have been a colony of Scots about 1670 under Colonel Ninian Beall, settled between the Potomac and the Patuxent, and gradually increased by successive additions. Through his influence a church was established at Patuxent in 1704, the members of which included several prominent Fifeshire families. Many other small Scottish colonies were settled on the eastern shore of Maryland and Virginia, particularly in Accomac, Dorchester, Somerset, Wicomico, and Worcester counties. To minister to them the Rev. Francis Makemie and the Rev. William Traill were sent out by the Presbytery of Laggan in Ulster. Upper Marlborough, Maryland, was founded by a company of Scottish immigrants and were ministered to by the Rev. Nathaniel Taylor, also from Scotland.

Two shiploads of Scottish Jacobites taken at Preston in 1716 were sent over in the ships *Friendship* and *Good Speed* to Maryland to be sold as servants. The names of some of these sufficiently attest their Scottish origin, as, Dugall Macqueen, Alexander Garden, Henry Wilson, John Sinclair, William Grant, Alexander Spalding, John Robertson, William MacBean, William McGilvary, James Hindry, Allen Maclien, William Cummins, David Steward, John MacIntire, David Kennedy, John Cameron, Alexander Orrach [Orrock?], Finloe MacIntire, Daniel Grant, etc. Another batch taken in the Rising of the '45 and also shipped to Maryland include such names as John Grant, Alexander Buchanan, Patrick Ferguson, Thomas Ross, John Cameron, William Cowan, John Bowe, John Burnett, Duncan Cameron, James' Chapman. Thomas Claperton, Sanders Campbell, Charles Davidson, John Duff, James Erwyn, Peter Gardiner, John Gray, James King, Patrick Murray, William Melvil, William Murdock, etc.

A strong infusion of Scottish blood in New York State came through settlements made there in response to a proclamation issued in 1735 by the Governor, inviting "loyal protestant Highlanders" to settle the lands between the Hudson River and the northern lakes. Attracted by this offer Captain Lauchlin Campbell of Islay, in 1738-40, brought over eighty-three families of Highlanders to settle on a grant of thirty thousand acres in what is now Washington County. "By this immigration," says E. H. Roberts, "the province secured a much needed addition to its population, and these Highlanders must have sent messages home not altogether unfavorable, for they were the pioneers of a multitude whose coming in successive years were to add strength and thrift and intelligence beyond the ratio of their numbers to the communities in which they set up their homes." Many Scottish immigrants settled in the vicinity of Goshen, Orange County, in 1720, and by 1729 had organized and built two churches. A second colony arrived from the north of Ireland in 1731. At the same time as the grant was made to Lauchlin Campbell, Lieutenant-Governor Clarke granted to John Lindsay, a Scottish gentleman, and three associates, a tract of eighty thousand acres in Cherry Valley, in Otsego County. Lindsay afterwards purchased the rights of his associates and sent out families from Scotland and Ulster to the valley of the Susquehanna. These were augmented by pioneers from Londonderry, New Hampshire, under the Rev. Samuel Dunlop, who, in 1743 established in his own house the first classical school west of the Hudson. Ballston in Saratoga County was settled in 1770 by a colony of Presbyterians who removed from Bedford, New York, with their pastor, and were afterwards joined by many Scottish immigrants from Scotland, Ulster, New Jersey, and New England. The first Presbyterian Church was organized in Albany in 1760 by Scottish immigrants who had settled in that vicinity.

Sir William Johnson for his services in the French War (1755-58) received from the Crown a grant of one hundred thousand acres in the Mohawk Valley, near Johnstown, which he colonized with Highlanders in 1773-74.

In New York City about the end of the eighteenth century there was a colony of several hundred Scottish weavers, mainly from Paisley. They formed a community apart in what was then the village of Greenwich. In memory of their old home they named the locality "Paisley Place." A view of some of their old dwellings in Seventeenth Street between Sixth and Seventh Avenues, as they existed in 1863, is given in Valentine's *Manual* for that year.

Although many Scots came to New England and New York they never settled there in such numbers as to leave their impress on the community so deeply as they did in New Jersey, Pennsylvania, Delaware, and the south. There were Presbyterian churches in Lewes, Newcastle (Delaware), and Philadelphia previous to 1698, and from that time forward the province of Pennsylvania was the chief centre of Scottish settlement both from Scotland direct and by way of Ulster. By 1720 these settlers had reached the mouth of the Susquehanna, and three years later the present site of Harrisburg. Between 1730 and 1745 they settled the Cumberland Valley and still pushing westward, in 1768-69 the present Fayette, Westmoreland, Allegheny, and Washington counties. In 1773 they penetrated to and settled in Kentucky, and were followed by a stream of Todds, Flemings, Morrisons, Barbours, Breckinridges, McDowells, and others. By 1790 seventyfive thousand people were in the region and Kentucky was admitted to the Federal Union in 1792. By 1779 they had crossed the Ohio River into the present state of Ohio. Between the years 1730 and 1775 the Scottish immigration into Pennsylvania often reached ten thousand a year.

SOME PROMINENT SCOTS AND SCOTS FAMILIES

Lord Bacon expressed his regret that the lives of eminent men were not more frequently written, and added that, "though kings, princes, and great personages be few, yet there are many excellent men who deserve better fate than vague reports and barren elegies." Of no country is this more true than the United States. An examination of the innumerable early biographical dictionaries with which the shelves of our public libraries are cumbered, will show that the bulk of the life sketches of the individuals therein commemorated are vague and unsatisfactory. In nearly every case little or no information is given of the parentage or origin of the subject, and indeed one work goes so far as to say that such information is unnecessary, the mere fact of American birth being sufficient. However pleasing such statements may be from an ultra patriotic viewpoint it is very unsatisfactory from the biological or historical side of the question, which is undoubtedly the most important to be considered. The neglect of these items of origin, etc., makes the task of positively identifying certain individuals as of Scottish origin or descent a very difficult one. One may feel morally certain that a particular individual from his name or features (if there be a portrait) is of Scottish origin, but without a definite statement to that effect the matter must in most cases be left an open question. One other cause of uncertainty, and it is a very annoying one, is the careless method of many biographers in putting down a man's origin as "Irish," "from Ireland," "from the north of Ireland," etc., where they clearly mean to state that the individual concerned is descended from one of the many thousands of Scots who settled in Ulster in the seventeenth and eighteenth centuries. Notwithstanding this uncertainty the proportion of men of undoubted Scottish origin who have reached high distinction, and whose influence has had such far reaching scope in the United States, is phenomenal. "Let anyone," says Dinsmore, "scrutinize the list of names of distinguished men in our annals; names of men eminent in public life from President down; men distingushed in the Church, in the Army, in the Navy, at the Bar, on the Bench, in Medicine and Surgery, in Education, trade, commerce, invention, discovery—in any and all of the arts which add to the freedom, enlightenment, and wealth of the world, and the convenience and comfort of mankind; names which have won luster in every honorable calling—let him scrutinize the list" and he will be astonished to find how large a proportion of these names represent men of Scottish birth or Scottish descent. In these pages it is obviously impossible to mention every Scot who has achieved distinction—to do so would require a large biographical dictionary. We can here only select a few names in each class from early colonial times to the present day.

The most famous family of Colonial times was that of the Livingstons of Livingston Manor, famed alike for their ability and their patriotism. The first of the family in America was Robert Livingston (1654-1725), born at Ancrum, Roxburghshire, who came to America about 1672. He married Alida (Schuyler) Van Rensselaer. His eldest son, Philip (1686-1749), second Lord of the Manor, succeeded him and added greatly to the family wealth and lands by his business enterprise. Peter Van Brugh Livingston (1710-92), second son of Philip, was President of the first Provincial Congress. Another son, Philip (1716-78), was Member of the General Assembly for the City of New York, Member of Congress in 1774 and 1776, and one of the Signers of the Declaration of Independence. A third son was William (1723-90), Governor of New Jersey. Other prominent members of this family were Robert R. Livingston (1746-1813), and Edward (1764-1836). The former was Member of the Continental Congress, Chancellor of the State of New York (1777-1801), Secretary of Foreign Affairs (1781-83), Minister to France (1801-05), and Negotiator of the Louisiana Purchase (1803). He administered the oath of office to George Washington on his assuming the office of President. Edward was Member of Congress from New York (1795-1801), Mayor of New York City (1801-03), Member of Congress from Louisiana (1823-29), United States Senator (1829-31), Secretary of State (1831-33), and Minister to France (1833-35). Robert Fulton, the inventor, married a daughter of the Livingstons and thus got the necessary financial backing to make the *Clermont* a success. A sister of Edward was married to General Montgomery of Quebec fame, another to Secretary of War Armstrong, and a third to General Morgan Lewis.

The Bells of New Hampshire descended from John Bell, the Londonderry settler of 1718, gave three governors to New Hampshire and one to Vermont. Luther V. Bell, formerly Superintendent of the McLean Asylum, Somerville, Massachusetts, was another of his descendants. The McNutts of Londonderry, New Hampshire, are descended from William McNaught, who settled there in 1718. The McNaughts came originally from Kilquhanite in Galloway. The Bean family, descended from John Bean who came to America in 1660, were pioneers in new settlements in New Hampshire and Maine, and bore the burden of such a life and profited by it. About one hundred of t' .m were soldiers in the Revolutionary War. The Macdonough family of Delaware is also of Scottish descent. Thomas Macdonough, the famous naval officer, was of the third generation in this country. The Corbit family of Delaware are descended from Daniel Corbit, a Quaker born in Scotland in 1682. The Forsyths of Georgia are descended from Robert Forsyth, born in Scotland about 1754, who entered the Congressional Army and became a Captain of Lee's Light Horse in 1776. The Forsyths of New York State trace their descent to two brothers from Aberdeenshire (John and Alexander). The bulk of the Virginia Gordons appear to have been from Galloway.

Alexander Breckenridge, a Scot, came to America about 1728, settling in Pennsylvania and later in Virginia. One of his sons, Robert, was an energetic Captain of Rangers during the Indian wars, and died before the close of the Revolutionary War. By his second wife, also of Scottish descent, he had several sons who achieved fame and success. One of these sons, John Breckenridge (1760-1808), became Attorney-General of Kentucky in 1795; served in the state legislature 1797-1800; drafted the famous Kentucky resolutions in 1798; was United States Senator from Kentucky (1801-05) and Attorney-General in Jefferson's Cabinet from 1805 till his death. Among the sons of John Breckenridge were Robert Jefferson Breckenridge (1800-71), clergyman and author, and Joseph Cabell Breckenridge. John Cabell Breckenridge, son of Joseph C. Breckenridge, was Vice-President of the United States (1857-61), candidate of the Southern Democrats for President in 1860, General in the Confederate Armies (1862-64), Confederate Secretary of War till 1865. Joseph Cabell Breckenridge (b. 1840), son of Robert J. Breckenridge, also served with distinction in the Civil War, and took an active part in the Santiago campaign during the Spanish-American War. Henry Breckenridge (b. 1886), son of Joseph C. Breckenridge, was Assistant Secretary of War, and served with the American Expeditionary Forces in the Argonne. William Campbell Preston Breckenridge (1837-1904), son of Robert J. Breckenridge, was Member of the Forty-ninth Congress.

The descendants of James McClellan, kin of the McClellans of Galloway, Scotland, who was appointed Constable at the town meeting held in Worcester in March, 1724, have written their name large in the medical and military annals of this country. Some of his descendants are noticed under Physicians. The most famous of the family was General George Brinton MacClellan (1826-85), Major-

General in the United States Army during the Civil War, unsuccessful candidate of the Democratic Party for President in 1864, and Governor of New Jersey from 1878 to 1881. The General's son, George B. McClellan (b. 1865), was Mayor of New York (1903 and 1905) and is now a Professor in Princeton. James Bulloch, born in Scotland c. 1701, emigrated to Charleston, South Carolina, c. 1728. In the following year he married Jean Stobo, daughter of the Rev. Archibald Stobo, and was the first ancestor of the late President Roosevelt's mother. His son, Archibald Bulloch (d. 1777), was Colonial Governor of Georgia and Commander of the State's forces in 1776-77, and signed the first Constitution of Georgia as President. He would have been one of the Signers of the Declaration of Independence had not official duties called him home. A descendant of his, James Dunwoody Bulloch, uncle of the late President Roosevelt, was Lieutenant in the Confederate Navy and Confederate States Naval Agent abroad. Irvine S. Bulloch, another uncle of Roosevelt's, was Sailing Master of the Alabama when in battle with the U. S. S. Kearsarge. Another of this family was William B. Bulloch (1776-1852), lawyer and State Senator of Georgia. The Chambers family of Trenton, New Jersey, are descended from two brothers, John and Robert Chambers, who came over in the ship *Henry and Francis* in 1685.

In the eighteenth century many natives of Dumfriesshire emigrated to the American colonies, and of these perhaps the most prominent were those descended from John Johnston of Stapleton, Dumfriesshire, an officer in a Scottish regiment in the French service. His second son, Gabriel, became Governor of North Carolina. In the house of the Governor's brother, Gilbert, it is stated that General Marion signed the commission for the celebrated band known as "Marion's Men." Among the more prominent descendants of Gilbert Johnston are: (1) James, who became a Colonel on the staff of General Rutherford during the Revolution and served in several engagements; (2) William, M.D., who married a daughter of General Peter Forney, and died in 1855. This William had five sons: (1) James, a Captain in the Confederate Army; (2) Robert, a Brigadier-General; (3) William, a Colonel; (4) Joseph Forney, born in 1843, Captain in the Confederate Army, Governor of Alabama from 1896 to 1900, and United States Senator for Alabama in 1907; (5) Bartlett, an officer in the Confederate Navy. Samuel Johnston, a nephew of Gilbert's, was the Naval Officer of North Carolina in 1775, Treasurer during the Revolution, and Governor of North Carolina from 1787 to 1789, President of the Convention that finally adopted the State Constitution, and first Senator elected by his state in the United States Congress in 1789. His son, James, was the largest planter in the

United States on his death in 1865. Gilbert's brother Robert, was an attorney and civil engineer. His son, Peter, served as Lieutenant in the legion which Colonel Henry Lee recruited in Virginia, and after the war became Judge of the South-Western Circuit in Virginia, and Speaker of the Virginia House of Delegates. He married Mary Wood, a niece of Patrick Henry. Their eighth son, Joseph Eccleston Johnston, born in 1807, graduated from West Point in 1829, served in the Federal Army in all its campaigns, up to the time of the Civil War. Although holding the rank of Lieutenant-Colonel and Quarter-Master-General, he resigned and joined the Confederate Army, and rendered brilliant service in its ranks. Another eminent individual of this name was General Albert Sydney Johnston, the son of a physician, John Johnston, the descendant of a Scottish family long settled in Connecticut. Christopher Johnston (1822-1891), a descendant of the Poldean branch of the Annandale Johnstons, was professor of surgery in the University of Maryland. His son, also named Christopher (d. 1914), graduated M.D., practised for eight years, studied ancient and modern languages, and eventually became Professor of Oriental History and Archaeology in Johns Hopkins University. He was one of the most distinguished Oriental scholars this country has produced.

Alexander Hamilton (1757-1804), one of the founders of the Republic, served with distinction in the Revolutionary War, but it was as a Statesman of the highest ability that he acquired his great fame. He was one of the most prominent Members of the Continental Congress (1782-83), of the Constitutional Convention in 1787, and Secretary of the Treasury (1789-95). He was born in the West Indies, the son of a Scots father and a French mother.

Thomas Leiper (1745-1825), born in Strathaven, Lanarkshire, emigrated to Maryland in 1763, was one of the first to favor separation from the mother country, and raised a fund for open resistance to the Crown.

Robert Stuart (1785-1848), pioneer and fur-trader, born at Callander, Perthshire, a grandson of Rob Roy's bitterest enemy. In 1810, in company with his uncle, John Jacob Astor, and several others, he founded the fur-trading colony of Astoria. His share in this undertaking is fully described in Washington Irving's *Astoria*. In 1817 Stuart settled at Mackinac as agent of the American Fur Company, and also served as Commissioner for the Indian tribes. General George Bartram, of Scottish parentage, was one of the "Committee of Correspondence" appointed to take action on the "Chesapeake Affair" in 1807, when war with Britain seemed imminent, and was active in military affairs during the war of 1812. Allan Pinkerton (1819-84), born in the Gorbals, Glasgow, organized the United States

Secret Service Division of the United States Army in 1861, discovered the plot to assassinate President Lincoln on his way to his inauguration in 1861, and also broke up the "Molly Maguires," etc. William Walker (1824-60), the filibuster, was born in Tennessee of Scots parentage. Rev. George Keith, a native of Aberdeen, became Surveyor-General of New Jersey in 1684. He founded the town of Freehold and marked out the dividing line between East and West Jersey. In 1693 he issued the first printed protest against human slavery, "An Exhortation & Caution to Friends concerning Buying and Keeping of Negroes," New York, 1693. James Alexander (1690-1756), a Scot, was disbarred for attempting the defense of John Peter Zenger, the printer, in 1735. Along with Benjamin Franklin he was one of the founders of the American Philosophical Society. Andrew Hamilton (1676-1741), the most eminent lawyer of his time, Attorney-General of Pennsylvania, and chief Commissioner for building Independence Hall in Philadelphia, was born in Scotland. For his championship of the freedom of the press and his successful defence of Zenger he was hailed by Governor Morris as "the day-star of the Revolution." His son James Hamilton, was the first native-born Governor of Pennsylvania and Mayor of Philadelphia. James Breghin or Brechin, Missionary, born in Scotland, took a prominent part in the affairs of Virginia (1705-19) and was an active supporter of Commissary Blair. Charles Anderson, another Missionary, probably a graduate of Aberdeen, served in Virginia from 1700 to 1719, was also a supporter of Blair. James Graham, first Recorder of the city of New York (1683-1700) and Speaker of Assembly (1691-99) was born in Scotland. Thomas Gordon (d. Perth Amboy, 1722), born in Pitlochrie, was Attorney-General of the Eastern District (1698), Chief Secretary and Registrar in 1702, later Speaker of Assembly, and in 1709 Chief Justice and Receiver-General and Treasurer of the province. Alexander Skene, who previously held office in Barbadoes, settled in North Carolina about 1696. In 1717 he was Member of Council and Assistant to the Judge of Admiralty to try a number of pirates. In 1719 he was elected Member of the New House of Assembly and became leader of the movement for the Proprietary Government. He was "looked upon as a man that understood public affairs very well." Major Richard Stobo (1727-c. 1770), a native of Glasgow, served in the Canadian campaign against the French. It was he who guided the Fraser Highlanders up the Heights of Abraham. Archibald Kennedy (c. 1687-1763), a relative of the Earl of Cassilis, was Collector of Customs of the Port of New York and Member of the Provincial Council. In his letters to headquarters and in his reports he urged the importance of the American Colonies to the mother country and advocated measures which, if carried out, would undoubtedly have strengthened their loyalty and added to their wealth and prosperity. Alexander Barclay, grandson of the Apologist of the Quakers, was Comptroller of the Customs under the Crown in Philadelphia from 1762 till his death in 1771. William Ronald, a native of Scotland, was a delegate in the Virginia Convention of 1788. His brother, General Andrew Ronald, was one of the Counsel representing the British merchants in the so-called British Debts Case. William Houston, son of Sir Patrick Houston, was a Delegate to the Continental Congress (1784-87) and a Depute from Georgia to the Convention for revising the Federal Constitution. His portrait, as well as that of his brother's, was destroyed by fire during the Civil War. Sir William Dunbar (c. 1740-1810), a pioneer of Louisiana, held important trusts under the Federal government and was a correspondent of Thomas Jefferson. Rev. Henry Patillo (1736-1801), born in Scotland, advocated separation from the mother country on every possible occasion, and was a Member of the Provincial Council in 1775. John Dickinson (1732-1808), Member of the Continental Congress of 1765, of the Federal Convention of 1787, and President of Pennsylvania (1782-85), was also the founder of Dickinson College, Carlisle, Pennsylvania. The Dickinsons came from Dundee in early colonial times. John Ross, purchasing agent for the Continental Army, was born in Tain, Ross-shire. He lost about one hundred thousand dollars by his services to his adopted country, but managed to avoid financial shipwreck. John Harvie, born at Gargunnock, died 1807, was Member of the Continental Congress (1777), signer of the Articles of Confederation the following year, and in 1788 was appointed Secretary of the Commonwealth. John McDonnell (1779-1846), born in Scotland, was in business in Detroit in 1812, and "thoroughly Americanized." He opposed the British commander's orders after the surrender of Hull, and redeemed many captives from the Indians. Became Member of State Constitutional Convention (1835), State Senator (1835-37), and Collector of the Port of Detroit (1839-41). John Johnstone Adair (b. 1807), graduate of Glasgow University, settled in Michigan, filled several important positions and became State Treasurer, State Senator, and Auditor General. Colonel James Burd (1726-93), born at Ormiston, Midlothian, took part with General Forbes in the expedition to redeem the failure of Braddock. General John Forbes (1710-59), born in Pittencrieff, Fifeshire, was founder of Pittsburgh. He was noted for his obstinacy and strength of character, and may have been the prototype of the Scotsman of the prayer: "Grant, O Lord, that the Scotchman may be right; for, if wrong,

he is eternally wrong." Captain William Bean was the first white
man to bring his family to Tennessee. His son, Russell Bean, was
the first white child born in the state. His descendant, Dr. James
Bean, died in a snowstorm on Mont Blanc while collecting specimens
for the Smithsonian Institution.

George Rogers Clark (1752-1818), to whose prowess is due the possession of the territory Northwest of the Ohio, secured by the peace
of 1783, was of Scottish descent. David Crockett (1786-1836), was
most probably of the same origin, though vaguely said to be "son of
an Irishman." The name is distinctly Scottish (Dumfriesshire).
Samuel McDowell (1735-1817), took an active part in the movement
leading to the War of Independence and was President of the first
State Constitutional Convention of Kentucky (1792). Colonel James
Innes, born in Canisbay, Caithness, was appointed Commander-in-
Chief of all the forces in the expedition to the Ohio in 1754 by Governor Dinwiddie.

Isaac Magoon, a Scot, was the first settler of the town of Scotland
(c. 1700), and gave it the name of his native country. Dr. John
Stevenson, a Scot, pioneer merchant and developer of Baltimore,
if not indeed its actual founder, was known as the "American Romu-
lus." George Walker, a native of Clackmannanshire, pointed out the
advantages of the present site of the Capital of the United States, and
George Buchanan, another Scot, laid out Baltimore town in 1730.
John Kinzie (1763-1828), the founder of Chicago, was born in Canada of Scottish parentage, the son of John MacKenzie. It is not
known why he dropped the "Mac." Samuel Wilkeson (1781-1848),
the man who developed Buffalo from a village to a city, was of Scottish descent. Alexander White (1814-72), born in Elgin, Scotland,
was one of the earliest settlers of Chicago and did much to develop
the city. Major Hugh McAlister, who served in the Revolutionary
War, later founded the town of McAlisterville, Pennsylvania, was of
Scots parentage. James Robertson (1742-1814), founder of Nashville, Tennessee, was of Scottish origin. His services are ranked next
to Sevier's in the history of his adopted state. Walter Scott Gordon
(1848-86), founder of Sheffield, Alabama, was the great-grandson of
a Scot. The town of Paterson, in Putnam county, New York, was
settled by Matthew Paterson, a Scottish stone-mason, in the middle of
the eighteenth century, and was named after him. Lairdsville, in
New York state, was named from Samuel Laird, son of a Scottish
immigrant, in beginning of the eighteenth century. Paris Gibson
(b. 1830), grandson of a Scot, founded and developed the town of
Great Falls.

SCOTS AS COLONIAL AND PROVINCIAL GOVERNORS

Of the colonial Governors sent from Britain to the American Colonies before the Revolution and of Provincial Governors from that time to 1789, a large number were of Scottish birth or descent. Among them may be mentioned the following:

NEW YORK. Robert Hunter, Governor (1710-19), previously Governor of Virginia, was a descendant of the Hunters of Hunterston, Ayrshire. He died Governor of Jamaica (1734). He was described as one of the ablest of the men sent over from Britain to fill public positions. William Burnet (1688-1729), Governor in 1720, was also Governor of Massachusetts (1720-1729). He was the eldest son of Gilbert Burnet, Bishop of Sarum. Smith, the historian of New York, calls him "a man of sense and polite breeding, a well bred scholar." John Montgomerie, Governor of New York and New Jersey (1728-31), was born in Scotland. John Hamilton, Governor (1736). Cadwallader Colden (1688-1776), Lieutenant-Governor (1761-1776), born in Duns, Berwickshire, was distinguished as physician, botanist, mathematician, and did much to develop the resources of the state. O'Callaghan in his "Documentary History of the State of New York," says: "Posterity will not fail to accord justice to the character and memory of a man to whom this country is most deeply indebted for much of its science and for many of its most important institutions, and of whom the State of New York may well be proud." John Murray, fourth Earl of Dunmore, Governor (1770-71), afterwards Governor of Virginia. James Robertson (1710-1788), born in Fifeshire, was Governor in 1780. Andrew Elliot, born in Scotland in 1728, was Lieutenant-Governor and administered the royalist government from 1781 to November, 1783.

NEW JERSEY. Robert Barclay of the Quaker family of Barclay of Ury was appointed Governor of East New Jersey in 1682, but never visited his territory. Lord Neil Campbell, son of the ninth Earl of Argyll, was appointed Governor in 1687, but meddled little in the affairs of the colony. Andrew Hamilton (c. 1627-1703), his deputy, born in Edinburgh, on Lord Neil Campbell's departure, became Acting Governor. He was an active, energetic officer, who rendered good service to the state, and organized the first postal service in the colonies. John Hamilton, son of Andrew, was Acting Governor for a time and died at Perth Amboy in 1746. William Livingston (1723-90), the "Don Quixote of New Jersey," grandson of Robert Livingston of Ancrum, Scotland, founder of the Livingston family in America, so famous in the history of New York State, was Governor from 1776 to 1790. William Paterson (1745-1806), of Ulster Scot birth, studied at Princeton, admitted to the New Jersey bar in November, 1767, Attorney-General in 1776, first Senator from New Jersey to first Congress (1789), succeeded Livingston as Governor (1790-92), and in 1793 became Justice of the Supreme Court. The city of Paterson is named after him.

PENNSYLVANIA. Andrew Hamilton, Governor (1701-03), was previously Governor of East and West Jersey. Sir William Keith (1680-1751), born in Peterhead, Aberdeenshire, Deputy Governor from 1717 to 1726. Patrick Gordon (1644-1736), Governor (1726-28). James Logan (1674-1751), born in County Armagh, son of Patrick Logan, of Scottish parentage, was Chief Justice of the Supreme Court of Pennsylvania from 1731 to 1739, and President of the Council (1736-38). He bequeathed his library of over two thousand volumes to Philadelphia, and they now form the "Loganian Library" in the Philadelphia Public Library. James Hamilton (c. 1710-1783), son of Andrew Hamilton, champion of the liberty of the press, was elected Member of the Provincial Assembly when but twenty years of age, and was re-elected five times. He was Deputy Governor 1748-54 and 1759-63. Robert Hunter Morris, of the famous New Jersey family of that name, Deputy Governor (1745-56). Joseph Reed, of Ulster Scot descent, Governor (1778-81). John Dickinson was President from 1782 to 1785.

DELAWARE. Dr. John McKinly (1721-96), first Governor of the state (1777), was of Ulster Scot birth. (All the above Governors of Pennsylvania except Reed also held the governorship of Delaware along with that of Pennsylvania.)

VIRGINIA. Robert Hunter (1707). (See above under New York.) Alexander Spotswood, Lieutenant-Governor (1710-22), a scion of the Spotswood of that Ilk. He was one of the ablest and most popular representatives of the crown authority in the Colonies and was the principal encourager of the growth of tobacco which laid the foundation of Virginia's wealth. Hugh Drysdale, Lieutenant-Governor (1722-26), was strongly opposed to the introduction of slavery into the colony. Commissary James Blair (1655-1743), President of Council (1740-41), was born in Scotland. Robert Dinwiddie, born in Glasgow in 1693, was Governor from 1751 to 1758. He recommended the annexation of the Ohio Valley and so secured that great territory to the United States. To him is also due the credit of calling George Washington to the service of his country. Dinwiddie county is named after him. John Campbell, Earl of Loudon (1705-82), Governor (1756-58), does not appear to have come to this colony. John Blair, Governor (1768), son of Dr. Archibald Blair and nephew of Rev. James Blair, the Commissary. Many of his descendants have distinguished themselves in the annals of Virginia. John Murray, fourth Earl of Dunmore, Governor (1771-75), was previously Governor of New York. Patrick Henry (1736-99), Governor (1776-79, 1784-86), was born in Hanover County, Virginia, of Scottish parentage, his father being a native of Aberdeen, his grandmother a cousin of William Robertson the historian. He became a lawyer in 1760 and in 1763 found his opportunity, when having been employed to plead against an unpopular tax, his great eloquence seemed suddenly to develop itself. This defence placed him at once in the front rank of American orators, and in 1765 he entered the Virginia House of Burgesses, immediately thereafter becoming leader in Virginia of the political agitation which preceded the Declaration of Independence. On the passage of the Stamp Act his voice was the first that rose in a clear, bold call to resistance, and in May, 1773, he assisted in procuring the passage of the resolution establishing a Committee of Correspondence for intercourse with the other colonies. In the Continental Congress which met in Philadelphia in 1774 he delivered a fiery and eloquent speech worthy of so momentous a meeting. In 1776 he carried the vote of the Virginia Convention for independence. He was an able administrator, a wise and far-seeing legislator, but it is as an orator that he will forever live in American history. William Fleming (1729-95), surgeon, soldier, and statesman, Councillor and Acting-Governor (1781), was born in Jedburgh, Roxburghshire.

NORTH CAROLINA. William Drummond, Governor of "Albemarle County Colony" (i. e., North Carolina), was a native of Perthshire, a strenuous upholder of the rights of the people, and r; nks as one of the earliest of American patriots. He took a prominent part in "Bacon's Rebellion" in 1676, "an insurrection that was brought about by the insolence and pig-headedness of Sir William Berkeley, then Governor of Virginia," and was executed the same year. Gabriel Johnston (1699-1752), Governor (1734-52), was born in Scotland, and held the Professorship of Oriental Languages in St. Andrews University before coming to the colonies. Johnston County is named after him. Matthew Rowan was President of Council and Acting Governor in 1753. Alexander Martin (1740-1807), was fourth and Acting Governor, 1782-84, and from 1789 to 1792. Samuel Johnston

(1733-1816), sixth Governor (1788-89), four years Senator, and Justice of the Supreme Court from 1800-1803. Bancroft says the movement for freedom was assisted by "the calm wisdom of Samuel Johnston, a native of Dundee, in Scotland, a man revered for his integrity, thoroughly opposed to disorder and revolution, if revolution could be avoided without yielding to oppression."

SOUTH CAROLINA. Richard Kirk, Governor (1684). James Glen, born in Linlithgow in 1701, Governor (1743-56). Lord William Campbell, third brother of the fifth Duke of Argyll, Governor (1775). John Rutledge (1739-1800), brother of Edward Rutledge the Signer, was President of South Carolina (1776-78) and first Governor (1779-82). He was later a delegate to the Constitutional Convention in 1787, Associate Justice of the United States Supreme Court (1789-91), Chief Justice of South Carolina (1791-95), and in 1795 appointed Chief Justice of the United States Supreme Court.

GEORGIA. William Erwin or Ewen, born in England in 1775. John Houston, son of Sir Patrick Houston, one of the prime instigators and organizers of the Sons of Liberty (1774), was Governor in 1774-76, 1778. His portrait was destroyed by fire during the Civil War. Houston County was named in his honor. Edward Telfair, born in the Stewartry of Kirkcudbright in 1735 and died at Savannah in 1807. When the revolutionary troubles commenced he earnestly espoused the side of the colonies, and became known locally as an ardent advocate of liberty. He was regarded as the foremost citizen of his adopted state, and his death was deeply mourned throughout the state.

FLORIDA. George Johnstone, a member of the family of Johnstone of Westerhall, was nominal Governor of Florida when that colony was ceded by Spain to Great Britain in 1763. He was one of the Commissioners appointed by the British government to try and restore peace in America in 1778.

SCOTS AND THE DECLARATION OF INDEPENDENCE

Presbyterians in the Colonies, being dissenters, were untrammeled and free to speak their mind in defence of their country's right, and history shows that they did not fail their opportunity: the doctrine of passive obedience never finding favor with them. In the Colonies the Presbyterian ministers claimed equal rights, religious freedom, and civil liberty. Their teaching had great influence, particularly in the South, and Patrick Henry of Virginia, David Caldwell, Dr. Ephraim Brevard, Rev. Alexander Craighead (d. 1766), and James Hall of North Carolina, the two Rutledges and Tennant of South Carolina, William Murdoch of Maryland, James Wilson and Thomas Craighead of Pennsylvania, Witherspoon of New Jersey, Read and McKean of Delaware, Livingston of New York, and Thornton of New Hampshire, with their associates had prepared the people for the coming conflict. In Maryland the lower house of the General Assembly was a fortress of popular rights and of civil liberty. Its resolutions and messages, beginning in 1733, and in an uninterrupted chain until 1755 continually declared "that it is the peculiar right of his Majesty's subjects not to be liable to any tax or other imposition but what is laid on them by laws to which they themselves are a party." These principles were reiterated and recorded upon the journals of every Assembly until 1771. The resolutions, addresses, and messages of the lower house during this period discuss with remarkable fullness and accuracy the fundamental principles of free government. and most of them emanated from William Murdoch, born in Scotland (c. 1720), who was one of the leading spirits and the directing force of the discussion. He led in the resistance to the Stamp Act and in other ways he united his colony in solid resistance to the attempt to levy taxes and imposts without their consent. In May, 1775, the General Synod of the Presbyterian Church met in Philadelphia and issued its famous "Pastoral Letter," which was sent broadcast throughout the Colonies, urging the people to adhere to the resolutions of Congress, and to make earnest prayer to God for guidance in all measures looking to the defense of the country. This powerful letter was also sent to the legislature in every colony.

Adolphus in his "History of England from the Accession of George III. to the Conclusion of Peace in 1783," published in London in 1802, declared that the Synod and their circular was the chief cause which led the Colonies to determine on resistance. There is no question that from the Scots Presbyterians and their descendants came many of the leaders in the struggle for independence, as Bancroft has well pointed out in the following words: "The first voice publicly raised in America to dissolve all connection with Great Britain came not from the Puritans of New England, nor the Dutch of New York, nor the planters of Virginia, but from the Scotch-Irish Presbyterians." Joseph Galloway (1730-1803), the Loyalist, than whom, says Ford, "there could be no better informed witness," "held that the underlying cause of the American Revolution was the activity and influence of the Presbyterian interest," and further, that "it was the Presbyterians who supplied the Colonial resistance a lining without which it would have collapsed." And Joseph Reed of Philadelpha, himself an Episcopalian, said: "The part taken by the Presbyterians in the contest with the mother country was indeed, at the time, often made a ground of reproach, and the connection between their efforts for the security of religious liberty and opposition to the oppressive measures of Parliament, was then distinctly seen. A Presbyterian loyalist was a thing unheard of." Parker, the historian, quotes a writer who says: "When the sages of America came to settle the forms of our government, they did but copy into every constitution the simple elements of representative republicanism, as found in the Presbyterian system. It is a matter of history that cannot be denied, that Presbyterianism as found in the Bible and the standards of the several Presbyterian churches, gave character to our free institutions." Ranke, the German historian, declared that "Calvin was the founder of the American Government;" and Gulian C. Verplanck of New York, in a public address, traced the origin of our Declaration of Independence to the National Covenant of Scotland. Chief Justice Tilghman (1756-1827) stated that the framers of the Constitution of the United States were through the agency of Dr. Witherspoon much indebted to the standards of the Presbyterian Church of Scotland in molding that instrument,

SCOTS AS SIGNERS OF THE DECLARATION OF INDEPENDENCE

Of the fifty-six Signers of the Declaration of Independence, no less than nine can be claimed as directly or indirectly of Scottish origin. Edward Rutledge (1749-1800), the youngest Signer, was a son of Dr. John Rutledge who emigrated from Ulster to South Carolina in 1735. The Rutledges were a small Border clan in Roxburghshire. William Hooper (1742-1790), was the son of a Scottish minister, who was born near Kelso and died in Boston in 1767. Hooper early displayed marked literary ability and entered Harvard University when fifteen years of age. At twenty-six he was one of the leading lawyers of the colony of North Carolina. George Ross (1730-79), was also of Scottish parentage. His nephew's wife, Elizabeth (Griscom) Ross (1752-1832), better known as "Betsy Ross," was maker of the first national flag. Matthew Thornton (1714-1803), the distinguished New Hampshire statesman and physician, was brought to this country from the north of Ireland by his father when about three years of age. He accompanied the expedition against Louisburg in 1745, was President of the Provincial Convention in 1775 and Speaker in January, 1776. In September, 1776, he was elected to Congress, and in November following signed the Declaration of Independence, although he had not been one of the framers. Thomas McKean (1734-1817), was a great-grandson of William McKean of Argyllshire who moved to Ulster about the middle of the seventeenth century. He was a member of Congress from Delaware (1774-83), Chief Justice of Pennsylvania (1777-99), and Governor of the state from 1799 to 1808. George Taylor (1716-81), described as the son of a clergyman and "born in Ireland," was most probably an Ulster Scot. He was a member of the Provincial Assembly of Pennsylvania from 1764 to 1770 and again in 1775. James Wilson (1742-1798), whose fame was to become as wide and lasting as the nation, was born in St. Andrews, the old university city of Fifeshire. He was a Delegate to Congress from Pennsylvania in 1776, Member of the Constitutional Convention of 1787, and Associate Justice of the United States Supreme Court from 1789 till his death. He strongly advocated independence as the only possible means of escape from the evils which had brought the various commonwealths into such a state of turmoil and dissatisfaction. Philip Livingston (1716-1778), grandson of Robert Livingston, the first of the American family of the name, was Member of Congress from New York in 1776. "His life was distinguished for inflexible rectitude and devotion to the interests of his country."

Last but greatest of all to be mentioned is the Rev. John Witherspoon (1722-94). Born in Yester, Scotland, educated in Edinburgh, minister in Paisley, he was called in 1768 to be President of the College of New Jersey, now Princeton University. He said he had "become an American the moment he landed." He took an active part in the public affairs of the colony of New Jersey, and in the convention which met to frame a constitution he displayed great knowledge of legal questions and urged the abolition of religious tests. In June, 1776, he was elected to the Continental Congress, and in the course of the debates he displayed little patience with those who urged half measures. When John Dickinson of Pennsylvania said the country was not ripe for independence, Witherspoon broke in upon the speaker exclaiming, "Not ripe, Sir! In my judgment we are not only ripe, but rotting. Almost every colony has dropped from its parent stem and your own province needs no more sunshine to mature it." He further declared that he would rather be hanged than desert his country's cause. One of his sons was killed at the battle of Germantown.

SCOTS IN THE PRESIDENCY

Of the twenty-nine Presidents of the United States five (Monroe, Grant, Hayes, Roosevelt, and Wilson) are of Scottish descent, and four (omitting Jackson who has been also claimed as Scottish by some writers) are of Ulster Scot descent, namely, Polk, Buchanan, Arthur, and McKinley. Jackson may possibly have been of Ulster Scot descent as his father belonged to Carrickfergus while his mother's maiden name, Elizabeth Hutchins, or Hutchinson, is Scottish. She came of a family of linen weavers. Benjamin Harrison might also have been included as he had some Scottish (Gordon) blood. His wife, Caroline Scott Harrison, was of Scottish descent.

James Monroe, fifth President, was descended from Andrew Monroe, who emigrated from Scotland in the middle of the seventeenth century. President Grant was a descendant of Matthew Grant, who came from Scotland to Dorchester, Mass., in 1630. George Hayes, ancestor of Rutherford B. Hayes, nineteenth President, was a Scot who settled in Windsor prior to 1680. Theodore Roosevelt was Dutch on his father's side and Scottish on his mother's. His mother was descended from James Bulloch, born in Scotland about 1701, who emigrated to Charleston, c. 1728, and founded a family which became prominent in the annals of Georgia. Woodrow Wilson's paternal grandfather, James Wilson, came from county Down in 1807. His mother, Janet (or Jessie) Woodrow, was a daughter of Rev. Thomas Woodrow, a native of Paisley, Scotland. James Knox Polk, eleventh President, was a great-great-grandson of Robert Polk or Pollok, who came from Ayrshire through Ulster. Many kinsmen of President Polk have distinguished themselves in the annals of this country. James Buchanan, fifteenth President, was of Ulster Scot parentage. Chester Alan Arthur, twenty-first President, was the son of a Belfast minister of Scottish descent. William McKinley, twenty-fifth President, was descended from David McKinley, an Ulster Scot, born about 1730, and his wife, Rachel Stewart. The surname McKinley in Ireland occurs only in Ulster Scot territory.

SCOTS AS VICE-PRESIDENTS

Of the Vice-Presidents of the United States six at least were of Scottish or Ulster Scot descent.

John Caldwell Calhoun (1782-1850), of Scottish descent on both sides. Previous to becoming Vice-President he was Secretary of War in Monroe's cabinet, and later was Secretary of State in the cabinet of President Tyler. He was one of the chief instruments in securing the annexation of Texas. George Mifflin Dallas (1792-1864), son of Alexander James Dallas, Secretary of the Treasury, was Minister to Russia in 1837-39, and subsequent to his Vice-Presidency was Minister to Great Britain (1856-61). John Cabell Breckenridge (1821-75), of direct Scottish descent, was Vice-President from 1857-61, candidate for President in 1860, Major-General in the Confederate Army (1862-64), and Confederate Secretary of War (1864-65). Henry Wilson (1812-75), of Ulster Scot descent, had a distinguished career as United States Senator before his election to the Vice-Presidency (1873-75). His original name was Jeremiah Jones Colbraith (i. e., Galbraith). He was also a distinguished author, his most important work being the "History of the Rise and Fall of the Slave Power in America" (1872-75). Thomas Andrews Hendricks (1819-85), who held the Vice-Presidency only for a few months (March to November, 1885), was of Scottish descent on his mother's side. Adlai Ewing Stevenson (1835-1914) was Member of Congress from Illinois (1875-77), and First Assistant Postmaster-General (1885-89), previous to becoming Vice-President (1893-97).

SCOTS AS CABINET OFFICERS

WAR. William Harris Crawford (1772-1834), descended from David Crawford, who came from Scotland to Virginia, c. 1654. Secretary of War (1615-16), Secretary of the Treasury (1816-25), and save for an unfortunate attack of paralysis, would have been President in 1824. He was also United States Senator from Georgia (1807-13) and Minister to France (1813-15). John Bell (1797-1869), Secretary (1841), Senator (1847-59), and candidate of the Constitutional Union Party for President in 1860, was probably of Scottish descent. George Washington Crawford, Secretary of War, was also Governor of Georgia. Simon Cameron (1799-1889), of Scottish parentage or descent, Senator (1845-49), Secretary of War in cabinet of Lincoln (1861-62), United States Minister to Russia (1862-63), and again Senator (1866-77). James Donald Cameron (1833-1918), son of the preceding, was Secretary under Grant for a year and United States Senator from 1877 to 1897. Daniel Scott Lamont (1851-1905), journalist and Secretary under Cleveland, was of Ulster Scot origin.

TREASURY. George Washington Campbell (1768-1848), Secretary (1814), was also Minister to Russia (1810-20). Alexander James Dallas (1759-1817), Secretary (1814-16), was the son of a Scottish physician, Dr. Robert C. Dallas. During 1815-16 he also discharged the functions of Secretary of War. Had a distinguished career as a statesman. Louis McLane (1776-1857), son of Allen McLane, a Revolutionary soldier and Speaker of the Legislature of Delaware, had a distinguished career as Senator from Delaware (1827-29), Minister to Great Britain (1829-31), Secretary of the Treasury (1831-33), and Secretary of State (1833-34). His son, Robert Milligan McLane (1815-98), had a distinguished career as a diplomat. James Guthrie (1792-1869), Secretary in the cabinet of President Pierce (1853-57). Thomas Ewing (1789-1871), was United States Senator from Ohio (1831-37), Secretary of the Treasury (1841), Secretary of the Interior (1849-50). He traced his descent from Findlay Ewing, a native of Loch Lomond, who distinguished himself in the Revolution of 1688 under William of Orange. Hugh McCulloch (1808-95), descended from Hugh McCulloch, Bailie of Dornoch, Sutherlandshire, was Comptroller of the Currency (1863-65), Secretary of the Treasury

(1865-69, 1884-85). He funded the National Debt during his first term as Secretary. Charles Foster (1825-1904), Governor of Ohio (1880-84), was Secretary of the Treasury from 1891 to 1893. Franklin MacVeagh (b. 1837), of Scottish ancestry, also held the office under President Taft.

INTERIOR. Alexander Hugh Holmes Stuart (b. 1807), Secretary in President Fillimore's cabinet, was son of Archibald Stuart, a Scot who fought in Revolutionary War. Thomas Ewing is already referred to (under Treasury). Samuel Jordan Kirkwood, Secretary of the Interior under Garfield, was also three times Governor of Iowa.

NAVY. Benjamin Stoddert (1751-1813), Secretary (1798-1801), was grandson of a Scot. William Alexander Graham (1804-75), Secretary (1850), was also Governor of North Carolina. He projected the expedition to Japan under Commodore Perry. James Cochrane Dobbin (1814-57). Paul Morton (1857-1911), Secretary (1904-05), was said to be descended from Richard Morton, a blacksmith and ironmaster of Scottish birth, who came to America about the middle of the eighteenth century.

STATE. James Gillespie Blaine (1830-93), Secretary (1881, 1889-92) and unsuccessful candidate for President in 1884. John Hay (1838-1905), one of the ablest Secretaries of State (1898-1905) this country ever had, was also of Scottish descent. He also held several diplomatic posts in Europe (1865-70), culminating in Ambassador to Great Britain (1897-98).

AGRICULTURE. James Wilson (1835-1920), Secretary (1897-1913) under McKinley, Roosevelt, and Taft, was born in Ayrshire, Scotland. He was Regent of Iowa State University, and in 1891 was elected to the chair of Practical Agriculture in the College of Agriculture and Director of the State Experiment Stations. He was wonderfully successful in the expansion and administration of the "most useful public department in the world."

LABOR. William Bauchop Wilson, born in Blantyre, near Glasgow, Scotland, in 1862, Secretary-Treasurer of the United Mine Workers of America (1900-09); Member of Congress (1907-13), and Chairman of the Committee on Labor in the sixty-second Congress, Secretary of Labor (1913).

POSTMASTER-GENERAL. The first postal service in the Colonies was organized by Andrew Hamilton, a native of Edinburgh, who obtained a patent for a postal scheme from the British Crown 'in 1694. A memorial stone on the south-west corner of the New York Post Office at Thirty-third Street commemorates the fact. John Maclean (1785-1861), Postmaster-General from 1823 to 1829, was later Associate Justice of the United States Supreme Court of Ohio, and unsuccessful candidate for the Republican nomination for President in 1856 and again in 1860. He took part in the famous Dred Scott case, in which he dissented from Taney, maintaining that slavery had its origin merely in power and was against right. James Campbell (1812-93), of Ulster Scot parentage, Postmaster-General in the cabinet of President Pierce, made a record by reducing the rate of postage and introducing the registry system. Montgomery Blair (1813-83) was Postmaster-General in the cabinet of President Lincoln. Adlai Ewing Stevenson, Assistant Postmaster-General, later became Vice-President.

SCOTS IN THE SENATE

John Ewing Colhoun (1749-1802), Member of State Legislature of South Carolina and Senator from the same state (1801), was of the same family as John C. Calhoun. George Logan (1753-1821), a man of high scientific attainments, grandson of James Logan, Quaker Governor of Pennsylvania, went to France in 1798 with the design of averting war with that country, Senator from Pennsylvania (1801-07). John Rutherfurd (1760-1840) was grandson of Sir John Rutherfurd of Edgerston, Scotland. James Brown (1766-1835), Senator and Minister-Plenipotentiary to France, was of Scottish descent. Jacob Burnet (1770-1853), Jurist and Senator, was the grandson of a Scot. His father, William Burnet (1730-91), was a skilful physician and Member of Congress. John Leeds Kerr (1780-1844), lawyer and Senator, was the son of James Kerr of Monreith. Alexander Campbell (1779-1857), Senator, was of Argyllshire descent. Walter Lowrie (1784-1868), Senator (1819-35) and thereafter Secretary of the Senate for twelve years, was born in Edinburgh. His four sons all became prominent in law and theology. Simon Cameron (1799-1889), grandson of a Cameron who fought at Culloden. His ancestor emigrated to America soon after the '45 and fought under Wolfe against the French at Quebec. Simon Cameron was also for a time Secretary of War in Lincoln's Cabinet and Minister to Russia. He named his residence at Harrisburg "Lochiel." His brother James was Colonel of the New York Volunteers, the 79th Highlanders, in the Civil War. James Donald Cameron (b. 1833), son of Simon Cameron, was President of the Northern Central Railroad of Pennsylvania (1863-74), Secretary of War Under General Grant, and Senator from Pennsylvania. Charles E. Stuart (1810-87), Lawyer and Senator, was a descendant of Daniel Stuart who came to America before 1680. Stephen Arnold Douglas (1813-61), Senator and unsuccessful candidate of the Democratic party for the Presidency in 1860, was of Scottish origin. Joseph Ewing MacDonald (1819-91), who held a foremost place among constitutional lawyers and was Democratic candidate for Governor of Indiana in 1864, was of Scottish ancestry. Francis Montgomery Blair (1821-75), a descendant of Commissary Blair of Virginia, was Senator from Missouri (1871-73), and Democratic candidate for Vice-President in 1868. James Burnie Beck (1822-90), born in Dumfriesshire, was Member of Congress (1867-75) and Senator from 1876 to 1890. He served on many important committees. Joseph McIlvaine (1765-1826), United States Senator from 1823 to 1826, was grandson of a Scot. His father fought on the Colonial side in the Revolution. Randall Lee Gibson (1822-92), of Scottish ancestry, Major-General in the Confederate Army during the Civil War, was United States Senator from Louisiana from 1883 till his death. His grandfather, Randall Gibson, was one of the founders of Jefferson College, Mississippi. John Brown Gordon (1832-1904), Lieutenant-General in the Confederate Army, thirty-fifth Governor of Georgia and United States Senator, was grandson of a Scot. Marcus Alonzo Hanna (1837-1904) was also partly Scottish descent. Calvin Stewart Brice (1845-1898), Chairman of the Democratic Campaign Committee (1888) and Senator from Ohio (1891-97), claimed descent from Bruce of Kinnaird. Daniel Hugh McMillan (b. 1846), was much identified with the welfare of Buffalo. His grandfather was "John the Upright," arbiter of the Hollanders of the Mohawk Valley during the latter part of the eighteenth century. Alexander McDonald (d. 1903), Senator from Arkansas (1868-71), was the son of John McDonald who came to the United States in 1827, and was one of the first to discover and develop bituminous coal mines on the west branch of the Susquehanna River in Pennsylvania. John Lendrum Mitchell (1842-1904), grandson of John Mitchell, farmer of Aberdeenshire, was State Senator of Wisconsin, Member of Congress from Wisconsin (1891-93), and Senator from the same state (1893-99), was also noted as a capitalist. Samuel James Renwick MacMillan (d. 1897), Chairman of the Committee of Commerce, was of Covenanting descent.

SCOTS IN THE HOUSE OF REPRESENTATIVES

Only a very few names of Members of Congress of Scottish birth or descent can be dealt with here. Some additional names will be found in other sections of this work. William Houston (b. about 1755), son of Sir Patrick Houston, was a Member of the Continental Congress. John Morin Scott (1730-84), grandson of the second son of Sir John Scott of Ancrum was Brigadier-General of New York State troops at the Battle of Long Island and Member of Congress from 1779 to 1783. William Burnet (1730-91), of Scottish parentage, physician and Member of Congress. Among his sons the following are worthy of notice: Dr. William Burnet of New Jersey, Major Ichabod Burnet of Georgia, Jacob Burnet, pioneer of Ohio, and David G. Burnet, Provisional President of the Republic of Texas. William Crawford (1760-1823), Member of Congress from 1809 to 1817, was born in Paisley. William Fitzhugh Gordon (1787-1858), Member from Virginia (1829-35), of Scottish descent, is said to have been the originator of the Sub-Treasury system. The town of Gordonsville, Virginia, was named after him or after his family. Leonidas Felix Livingston (b. 1832), grandson of Adam Livingston from Scotland, who served in the Revolutionary War, was a Member of the Georgia Legislature and Member of Congress. John Louis Macdonald (b. 1838), newspaper editor, State Senator, etc., was born in Glasgow. James Buchanan (b. 1839) of Scottish descent, was Member from New Jersey to 49th, 50th, 51st and 52nd Congress. David Bremner Henderson (1840-1906), born at Old Deer, Aberdeenshire, served in the Civil War and lost a leg at Corinth, was Member from Iowa (1880-99), and Speaker of the House of Representatives (1899-1906). William Grant Laidlaw, born near Jedburgh, Scotland, in 1840, served in the Civil War and was Member of Congress from 1887 to 1891. John Edgar Reyburn (b. 1845), Member State Senate of Pennsylvania, Member of Congress 1890-1907; and James Fleming Stewart (1851-1904), were both of Scottish descent.

SCOTS IN THE JUDICIARY

As with the medical and theological professions the legal has shared the dominating influence of Scotland, and indeed it is perhaps not too much to say that much of the distinctive character of American jurisprudence is due to the influence of men of Scottish blood at the bench and bar. The second Chief Justice of the United States Supreme Court (John Rutledge) and two of the four original Associate Justices, Blair and Wilson, were of Scottish origin. The mother of John Marshall, the great Chief Justice, was of Scottish origin (Keith). Of fifty judges of the United States Supreme Court from 1789 to 1882, at least fifteen were of Scottish birth or descent. We have space here to deal with only a selection of the most prominent names.

Andrew Kirkpatrick (1756-1831), Chief Justice of New Jersey for twenty-one years, whose "decisions especially those on realty matters, show a depth of research, a power of discrimination, and a justness of reasoning which entitle him to rank among the first American jurists," was of Scottish parentage, descended from the Kirkpatricks of Dumfriesshire. His son, also named Andrew, was President Judge of the Court of Common Pleas of Essex County (1885-96) and United States District Judge (1896-1904). George Robertson (1790-1874), Chief Justice of Kentucky (1829-43), "whose name stands first in the list of great men who have occupied and adorned the Appellate bench of Kentucky," and who declined the offer of the governorship of Arkansas, was of Scottish ancestry. Robert Cooper Grier (1794-1870), Associate Justice of the Superior Court of Connecticut (1846-70) was of same origin. Eugenius Aristides Nisbet (1803-71), descended from Murdoch Nisbet, a Lollard of Kyle, after a brilliant career in the state legislature became Chief Justice of the Supreme Court of Georgia. Thomas Todd (1765-1826), Associate Justice of the Supreme Court (1807-26). The first Chief Justice of Delaware, William Killen (1722-1805), was born in the north of Ireland of Scottish parentage. John J. Milligan (1795-1875), grandson of a Scottish emigrant from Ayrshire, was Associate Justice of Delaware, and refused, on account of ill health, the portfolio of Secretary of the Interior in the cabinet of President Fillimore. Ellis Lewis

(1798-1871), Chief Justice of the Supreme Court of Pennsylvania (1855-57) was of Scottish descent. Alexander Addison (1759-1807), born in Scotland, became President Judge of the fifth judicial district of Pennsylvania under the constitution of 1770. Robert Hunter Morris, Lieutenant-Governor of Pennsylvania, was Chief Justice of New Jersey for twenty-one years. John McLean (1785-1861), Associate Justice, is noticed under Scots in the Presidential Cabinet; and William Paterson, Associate Justice (1793-1806), is mentioned under Colonial Governors. Samuel Nelson (1792-1873), Associate Justice of the Supreme Court, was of Ulster Scot descent. "His decisions have stood the test of time and the searching analysis of the most able lawyers." Thomas Douglas (1790-1853), first Chief Justice of Florida, was ot Scots ancestry. William Wallace Campbell (1806-81), great-grandson of an Ulster Scot, was distinguished as a jurist and as a historian of New York State. He was author of *Annals of Tryon County* (1831), *Border Warfare of New York* (1849), *Life and Writings of De Witt Clinton* (1849), etc. During a visit to Scotland in 1848 he was elected an honorary member of the Clan Campbell at a great gathering at Inveraray. Thomas Drummond (1809-90), grandson of a Scot from Falkirk, was Justice of the Illinois Supreme Court. John Archibald Campbell (1811-89), Associate Justice of the Supreme Court (1853-61), was Assistant Secretary of War in the Confederate Cabinet, and in 1865 took part in the "Hampton Roads Conference." John Wallace Houston (1841-95), Associate Justice of the Supreme Court of Delaware, was of Scots descent. His ancestors first settled in New York city, and Houston Street is named after one of them. Other Associate Justices of Delaware of Scottish descent are Charles Mason Cullen (1829-1903), and George Gray (b. 1840), Attorney-General (1879-85), United States Senator, Member of the Russo-Japanese Peace Commission of 1898, and Member of the Anthracite Coal Strike Commission of 1902. James Gilfillan (1829-94), born at Bannockburn, Stirlingshire, "a profound scholar, and as a jurist was distinguished for his ability, firmness, and absolute impartiality." William Joseph Robertson (1817-98), born in Virginia of Scottish parents, was Judge of the Supreme Court of Virginia and Judge of the Supreme Court of Appeals (1859). Thomas Sloan Bell (1800-61), of Scottish parentage, became President Judge of the Judicial District of the counties of Wayne, Pike, Carbon, and Monroe, in Pennsylvania, in 1855, and held many other important positions. Samuel Dana Bell, son of Samuel Bell, Governor of New Hampshire, was Chief Justice of the Supreme Court of New Hampshire (1859-64). Matthew Hall McAllister (1800-65), for several years Mayor of Savannah, Georgia, afterwards United States Circuit Judge of

California, LL. D. of Columbia University, was of Scottish ancestry. Thomas Ewing (1829-96), son of Thomas Ewing, Secretary of the Treasury, at the age of twenty-nine was elected first Chief Justice of the Supreme Court of Ohio. During the Civil War he took a conspicuous part and rose to the rank of General. William Harper (1790-1847), born in Antigua, Leeward Islands, of Scottish parents, was Chancellor of the University of South Carolina (1828-30, 1835-47) and Judge of the Court of Appeals of South Carolina (1830-35). John Bannister Gibson (1780-1853), Chief Justice of Pennsylvania, was of Ulster Scot descent. Harry Innes (1752-1816), of Scottish parentage, was one of the Commissioners appointed to draft a constitution for Kentucky, being chosen by Washington because of his integrity. He was also appointed first Chief Justice of Kentucky but declined the office. John Buchanan (1772-1844), of Scottish ancestry, was Chief Justice of Maryland, and Chief Justice of the Court of Appeals for thirty-seven years. His brother, Thomas, was associated with him on the bench. David Torrance (1840-1906), Chief Justice of the Supreme Court of Connecticut, was born in Edinburgh.

SCOTS AS AMBASSADORS

Some of those who have represented this country at foreign courts previously held office in the Cabinet or were Members of the Senate are noted under these headings:
John Graham (1774-1820), Minister-Plenipotentiary to Brazil (1819), was brother of George Graham, Acting Secretary of War in the cabinets of Madison and Monroe. Charles Johnston McCurdy (b. 1797), of Ulster Scot descent, was Minister to Austria (1851-52) and Justice of the Supreme Court. Miller Grieve (1801-78), born in Edinburgh, Representative in the Georgia Legislature, Chairman of Board of Trustees of Oglethorpe University, was Chargé d'Affaires at Copenhagen. William Hunter (1774-1849), of Scottish parentage, a scholar and linguist, United States Senator from Rhode Island (1812-20), was Minister-Plenipotentiary to Brazil in 1834. William Bradford Reed (1806-76) was Envoy-Extraordinary and Minister-Plenipotentiary to China. Lewis Davis Campbell (1811-82), Chairman Ways and Means Committee in the thirty-fourth Congress, was United States Minister to Mexico. Robert Milligan McLane (1815-98), son of Allen McLane, was United States Minister to China (1853-55), Mexico (1859-60), and France (1885-88). John M. Forbes (d. 1831), descendant of the Scottish family of Forbes, was Secretary of Legation to Buenos Ayres (1823) and Chargé d'Affaires (1825-31). James Hepburn Campbell (1820-95) Member of Congress and Minister to Sweden and Norway (1864-67). John Adam Kasson (1822-1910), descendant of Adam Kasson (1721) from Argyllshire, had a distinguished career, the list of honors held by him is long. Whitelaw Reid (1837-1912), one of the half dozen most distinguished representatives of this country abroad was of Scottish descent on both sides. Wayne MacVeagh (b. 1833), of Scottish origin, was United States Minister to Turkey (1870-71), Ambassador to Italy (1893-97), and was also Attorney-General under President Garfield. Thomas Barker Ferguson (b. 1841), diplomat and inventor, was great-grandson of James Ferguson who emigrated from Scotland at end of seventeenth century. He was Commissioner of Fish and Fisheries (1878-87), Envoy-Extraordinary and Minister-Plenipotentiary to Sweden and Norway (1893-97), etc. His grandfather was a

Member of the South Carolina Provincial Legislature and Member of the Council of Safety. Whiteside Godfrey Hunter, born in Londonderry in 1841, of Scottish ancestry, was a Member of Congress and Envoy-Extraordinary and Minister-Plenipotentiary to Guatemala and Honduras. Richard Renshaw Neill (b. 1845), was Secretary of United States Legation at Lima, Peru, and has been Chargé d'Affaires there eight different times. Hugh Anderson Dinsmore (b. 1850), of Ulster Scot origin, was Minister Resident and Consul General in Corea (1887-90) and later Member of Congress (1892-1906). John Wallace Riddle (b. 1864), held several diplomatic posts culminating in becoming Ambassador to Russia (1906-09). Thomas Cleland Dawson (b. 1865), son of a native of Clackmannan, was Secretary of the American Legation to Brazil (1897-1904), Minister Resident and Consul General to Santo Domingo (1904), and author of "South American Republics," a standard work (2 v. 1903-4). George Brinton McClellan Harvey the present Ambassador to Great Britain is descended from Stuart Harvey who came from Scotland in 1820.

SCOTS AS STATE GOVERNORS

MAINE. Robert Pinckney Dunlap (1794-1859), eighth governor, and Hugh Johnston Anderson (1801-81), fourteenth Governor (1844-47), were of Ulster Scot descent. Abner Coburn (1803-85), twenty-fourth Governor, was also most probably of Scottish or Ulster Scot descent.

NEW HAMPSHIRE. Jeremiah Smith, fourth Governor (1809-10), was of Ulster Scot parentage. His son, of the same name, was an Associate Justice of the Supreme Court of the state. Samuel Bell (1770-1850), a descendant of one of the Ulster Scot settlers of 1718, was three times elected Governor (1819-23) with little or no opposition. John Bell (1765-1836), his brother, was thirteenth Governor (1828-29). Joseph Morrill Harper (1789-1865), who served as acting Governor in 1831, was of Ulster Scot descent. Samuel Dinsmoor (1766-1835), sixteenth Governor (1831-33), a distinguished factor in the history of his state, was of Ulster Scot descent on both sides. His eldest son (1799-1869), also named Samuel, served as twenty-fourth Governor (1849-52). Noah Martin (1801-63), of Ulster Scot descent on both sides, was the twenty-fifth Governor. Charles Henry Bell (1823-93), son of Governor John Bell, was forty-first Governor of the state. John Butler Smith, forty-seventh Governor (1893-95), was a descendant of one of the settlers of 1718. John McLane (1852-1911) fifty-seventh Governor (1905-06), was born in Lennoxtown, Scotland. He was host at the Russian-Japanese Conference at Portsmouth.

VERMONT. Charles James Bell, fiftieth Governor (1905), was descended from one of the Londonderry, N. H., settlers of 1718. John Wolcott Stewart, thirty-third Governor (1870-72), was descended from Robert Stewart who went from Edinburgh to Londonderry, Ireland, and whose son was one of those who emigrated from there to Londonderry, N. H., in 1718. His grandfather fought in the Revolutionary War.

MASSACHUSETTS. William Claflin (1818-1905), twenty-third Governor, was a descendant of one of the Scots prisoners taken at the battle of Dunbar in 1650.

RHODE ISLAND. General Ambrose E. Burnside (1824-81), Governor (1867-69). William Gregory (1849-1901), forty-second Governor (1900-01), was of direct Scottish descent.

CONNECTICUT. George Payne McLean, forty-first Governor (1901-03), was of Scottish descent.

DELAWARE. Charles Polk (1788-1857), thirteenth Governor (1827-30), and President of the Constitutional Convention of his state in 1831, was of Ulster Scot descent. John P. Cochran (1809-98), twenty-sixth Governor (1875-79), was of the same origin.

PENNSYLVANIA. Thomas McKean, Governor (1799-1808), is already noticed under Signers of the Declaration of Independence. William Findlay (1768-1846), fourth Governor (1817-20), of Ulster Scot descent, was also United States Senator and Treasurer of the Mint at Philadelphia. William Freame Johnston (1802-72), Governor from 1848 to 1852, was of Scottish parentage. He did much to develop the oil region of Pennsylvania, and was also President of the Allegheny Valley Railroad. James Pollock (1810-90), Governor (1855-58). It was through his efforts that "In God we trust" was placed on the coinage. John White Geary (1819-73), Governor from 1867 to 1873, was of Ulster Scot descent.

MARYLAND. John Francis Mercer (1759-1821), eleventh Governor 1801-03), was a descendant of the Mercers of Aldie, Perthshire. Robert Bowie (1749-1818), twelfth and fifteenth Governor (1803-06, 1811-12), and Robert Milligan McLane (1815-98), forty-second Governor (1884-85), were of direct Scottish descent. Frank Brown, forty-fifth Governor (1892-96), was descended from Abel Brown who emigrated from Dumfries, c. 1730.

VIRGINIA. James Barbour (1776-1842) was eleventh Governor (1812-14). Barbour County, Florida, was named in his honor. David Campbell (1779-1859), twenty-first Governor (1837-40), was of Scottish descent on both sides. Thomas Walker Gilmer (1802-44), twenty-second Governor (1840-41), was a descendant of the Scottish physician, Dr. George Gilmer. John Mercer Patton (1797-1858), Lieutenant-Governor and acting Governor (1841), was son of Robert Patton who emigrated from Scotland. His mother was a daughter of Gen. Hugh Mercer. John Rutherford (1792-1865), twenty-third Governor (1841-42), was most probably of Scottish descent. William Ewan Cameron, thirty-sixth Governor (1882-86) descended from the Rev. John Cameron, a graduate of Aberdeen University, who came to America, c. 1770. Henry Carter Stuart (b. 1855), Governor (1914-18), descended from Archibald Stuart who fled from Scotland for political reasons and settled in Virginia in 1726.

WEST VIRGINIA. William Erskine Stevenson (1820-1883), second Governor (1869-71) was born of Ulster Scot parentage. William

Alexander Mac Corkle (b. 1857), eighth Governor (1893-97) is of Scottish descent. His grandfathers, Captain John MacCorkle and Captain John McNutt, fell at the battle of Cowpens, 1781.

NORTH CAROLINA. Nathaniel Alexander (1756-1808), thirteenth Governor (1805-07), was of Scottish descent. William Alexander Graham (1804-75), thirtieth Governor (1845-49), was son of Genr. Joseph Graham, a Revolutionary officer.· He was also Secretary of the Navy in 1850, and projected the expedition to Japan under Commodore Perry. Tod R. Caldwell (1818-74), fortieth Governor (1871-74), and David Lindsay Russell, forty-eighth Governor (1897-1901), were both of direct Scottish descent.

SOUTH CAROLINA. General William Moultrie, son of Dr. Moultrie, was Governor in 1785-87 and 1794-96. Edward Rutledge, tenth Governor (1798-1800), is already noticed under the Signers of the Declaration of Independence. "No measure of importance was adopted by the legislature without his taking part in it, while many originated with himself." Andrew Pickens, (1779-1838), nineteenth Governor (1816-18), was a son of Andrew Pickens, the noted Revolutionary general. John Geddes (1777-1828), twentieth Governor (1818-20), was of Scottish descent. Stephen Decatur Miller (1787-1838), twenty-fifth Governor (1828-30), also served as United States Senator. George McDuffie (1790-1851), twenty-eighth Governor, the greatest orator and statesman of Georgia, was of Scottish parentage on both sides. McDuffie County in Georgia is so named in his honor. Patrick Noble (1787-1840), thirtieth Governor (1838-40), was grandson of an Ulster Scot immigrant. Robert Kingston Scott (1826-1900), forty-fifth Governor (1868-72), was the grandson or great-grandson of a refugee from Culloden.

GEORGIA. David Brodie Mitchell (1766-1837), ninth Governor (1809-11, 1815-17), was born in Scotland. He was described as "a conscientious, cultured, and conservative man, of great energy, public spirit, and animated by the purest patriotism." George McIntosh Troup (1780-1856), the "Hercules of State Rights," fourteenth Governor (1823-27), was of Scottish descent on both sides. He was one of Georgia's most illustrious Chief Magistrates. A county in the state is named after him. John Forsyth (1780-1841), fifteenth Governor (1827-29), was also United States Secretary of State. George Rockingham Gilmer (1790-1859), sixteenth Governor (1829-31, 1837-39), was the grandson of a Scottish physician, Dr. George Gilmer. He was also Member of Congress.· He also wrote a work, "Georgians," 1855, containing much valuable matter relating to the early settlers of his state. Charles James McDonald (1793-1860), nineteenth Governor

(1839-43), and George Washington Crawford (1798-1872), twentieth Governor (1843-47), were both of Scottish descent. James Johnson, twenty-fifth Governor (1861), was grandson of a Scottish immigrant, He rendered great service to his state in its reconstruction after the war. Alexander Hamilton Stephens (1812-83), grandson of an adherent of Prince Charles Edward, was Vice-President of the Confederacy (1861-65), chief Confederate Commissioner in the Hampton Roads Conference in February, 1865. Member of Congress from Georgia (1873-82), Governor of the state (1883), and author of "The War Between the States" (1868-70) and of a "History of the United States" (1883). John Brown Gordon (1832-1904), thirty-fifth Governor (1886-90), was the great-grandson of one of seven brothers who emigrated from Scotland, all of whom served in the Revolutionary Army. As Governor his administration was faultless, and the New York Sun declared his inauguration "worthy of Thomas Jefferson."

FLORIDA. Francis Philip Fleming (b. 1841), fourteenth Governor (1889-93), was of Scottish descent. Alexander Walker Gilchrist. nineteenth Governor (1909), a descendant of Nimrod Gilchrist, who came from Glasgow in 1750.

ALABAMA. Israel Pickens (1780-1827), third Governor (1821-25), Democratic Member of Congress from North Carolina (1811-17), United States Senator (1826), was of Scottish descent. Reuben Chapman (1802-82), eleventh Governor (1847-49), was also of Scottish ancestry. Robert Miller Patton (1809-85), seventeenth Governor (1865-68), was Ulster Scot on his father's side and Scottish on his mother's. Robert Burns Lindsay, born in Dumfriesshire in 1824, a linguist and a scholar, educated at the University of St. Andrews, was nineteenth Governor (1870-72). George Smith Houston (1811-79), twenty-first Governor, and Joseph Forney Johnston (b. 1843), twenty-seventh Governor (1896-1900), were both of Scottish descent.

TENNESSEE. Joseph McMinn (d. 1824), fifth Governor (1815-21), was most probably of Scottish descent. Samuel Houston, seventh Governor (1827-28), is noticed under Texas. Neil S. Brown, fourteenth Governor (1847-49), was grandson of Angus Brown, a Scot who fought in the Revolutionary War under Gen. Francis Marion. William Bowen Campbell (1807-67), sixteenth Governor (1851-53), was also of Scottish descent. Benton McMillin (b. 1845), Governor (1899-1903), Envoy-Extraordinary and Minister-Plenipotentiary to Peru in 1913, of Ulster Scot descent.

KENTUCKY. John Adair (1797-1840), eighth Governor (1820-24), was of Scottish parentage. "His term was marked by great legislative activity for the promotion of education in the state, and by the abolition of imprisonment for debt." The state library was founded under his auspices. Adair county was so named in his honor. John Breathitt (1786-1834), Lieutenant-Governor (1828-32), and eleventh Governor (1832-34), was the son of a Scottish emigrant. "A man of high character and his public career irreproachable." Breathitt county was named after him. James Fisher Robinson (1800-92), twenty-second Governor, was of English and Scottish descent.

OHIO. Duncan McArthur (1772-1840), an early Governor (1830-32), was of Scottish ancestry. He also held the rank of General in the war of 1812. Jeremiah Morrow (1770-1852), Governor (1822-26), and Allen Trimble (1783-1870), Governor (1826-30), were both Ulster Scot descent. James E. Campbell (b. 1843), Governor (1890-92), was previously Member of Congress. James M. Cox (b. 1870), forty-sixth Governor (1913-15) is of Scottish ancestry.

INDIANA. Noah Noble, fifth Governor (1831-37), was grandson of a Scottish immigrant. David Wallace (1799-1859), sixth Governor (1837-40), and Samuel Bigger (1802-46), were also of Scottish ancestry. Thomas Andrews Hendricks, Governor from 1873 to 1877, is already noticed under Vice-Presidents.

MICHIGAN. Robert McClelland (1807-80), Governor (1851-53), afterwards Secretary of the Interior; and Austin Blair (1814-94), war Governor, who sent over 83,000 soldiers from his state during the Civil War, were both of Scottish ancestry.

WISCONSIN. The mother of Henry Dodge, first and fourth Governor (1836-41, 1845-48), was Anne Nancy Hunter, of Ulster Scot parentage. William E. Smith (1824-83), thirteenth Governor (1878-82), was born in Scotland.

ILLINOIS. William Lee Davidson Ewing (1795-1846), Senator and acting Governor (1834), was of Ulster Scot descent. Joseph Duncan (1794-1844), fifth Governor (1834-38), who greatly encouraged education in his state, was of Scottish ancestry. John Lourie Beveridge (b. 1824) fifteenth Governor, was grandson of a Scot who came to the United States about 1770. His "administration was vigorous, just, and impartial."

MISSISSIPPI. John J. McRae (1815-68), nineteenth Governor (1854-58), was of Scottish descent. William McWillie (1795-1869), twentieth Governor (1858-60), and Anselm Joseph McLaurin (b. 1848), thirty-second Governor (1896-1900), were both grandsons of Scots.

LOUISIANA. John McEnery (1833-91), nineteenth (unrecognized) Governor (1873), was of Scottish descent. Samuel Douglas McEnery

(b. 1837), brother of the preceding, was twenty-second Governor (1881-88). John Newton Pharr (1829-1903), elected Governor in 1896 but not seated on account of the negro question, was descended from Walter Pharr who came from Scotland in 1765.

MISSOURI.   Alexander McNair (1774-1826), first state Governor (1820-24), most probably was of Scottish birth or descent. Trusten Polk (1811-76), of same origin as President Polk, was eleventh Governor (1857). Benjamin Gratz Brown (1826-85), also of Scottish descent, was Governor from 1871 to 1873, and unsuccessful candidate for Vice-President in 1872.

IOWA.   John Chambers (1780-1852), second Governor of the territory of Iowa was of Scottish descent on both sides. James Wilson Grimes (1816-72), third Governor (1854-58), was of Ulster Scot descent. Samuel Jordan Kirkwood (1813-94), three times Governor of his state (1860-64, 1876-77), was descended from a brother of Captain Robert Kirkwood, a Delaware soldier of the Revolution. He was also Secretary of the Interior under Garfield. John Henry Gear (1825-1900), eleventh Governor (1878-82), Assitsant Secretary of United States Treasury (1892-93), and Senator (1895-1900), was of Scottish ancestry. Albert Baird Cummins, eighteenth Governor, of Ulster Scot ancestry.

MINNESOTA.   Alexander Ramsey, first territorial and second state Governor (1849-53, 1860-64), was grandson of an Ulster Scot who served in the Revolutionary War.

NEBRASKA.   James E. Boyd (b. 1834), eighth Governor (1891-92), was born in county Tyrone of Ulster Scot ancestry.

KANSAS.   John Alexander Martin (1839-89), ninth Governor (1885-89), was of Ulster Scot descent.

TEXAS.   Samuel Houston (1793-1863) was a descendant of John Houston who settled in Philadelphia in 1689. He was Member of Congress from Tennessee (1823-27), Governor of Tennessee (1827-28), and as Commander-in-chief of the Texans he defeated the Mexicans under Santa Anna in 1836 on the banks of the San Jacinto, and by this one blow achieved the independence of Texas. He was elected first President of the new republic in the same year, was re-elected in 1841, and in 1859 was elected Governor of the state. Houston, the capital of Harris County, Texas, was named in his honor. Peter Hansborough Bell (1812-98), third Governor (1849-53), was of Ulster Scot ancestry, as was also James Edward Ferguson (b. 1871). James Stephen Hogg, nineteenth Governor and Thomas Mitchell Campbell, twenty-third Governor, were of Scottish descent.

COLORADO.   Edward Moody McCook, fifth and seventh Governor

(1869-73, 1874-75), was of Scottish descent. He also served in the Civil War and attained the rank of Brigadier-General. James Benton Grant, tenth Governor (1883-85), was grandson of a Scottish immigrant. Jesse Fuller McDonald, twenty-third Governor (1905-07), a descendant of James McDonald who emigrated from Scotland early in the eighteenth century and settled in Maine.

WYOMING. Thomas Moonlight (1833-99), sixth territorial Governor (1887-90), was born in Forfarshire.

UTAH. Eli Houston Murray (b. 1841), Governor (1880-84), of Scottish ancestry.

IDAHO. John Henry Brady (b. 1862), eighth Governor (1910-11), is of Ulster Scot descent. David P. Thompson, ninth Governor of the state (1874-76), also of Ulster Scot descent, built the first railroad in Oregon, and was twice Mayor of Portland.

SOUTH DAKOTA. Corie Isaac Crawford, sixth Governor (1907-08) is of Ulster Scot descent.

CALIFORNIA. John McDougall (1818-66) was Lieutenant-Governor (1849) and afterwards Governor. Peter Hardeman Burnett (b. 1807) was first Governor of the state (1849-51). Both were of Scottish origin.

OREGON. James Shields, first territorial Governor (1848), was born in Dungannon, County Tyrone, of Ulster Scot parentage. George Abernethy (1807-77), territorial Governor (1845-49), was born in New York city of Scottish parentage. "As a governor he was patriotic, efficient, and unselfish."

SCOTS IN THE ARMY

REVOLUTION. Alexander MacDougall (1731-86), born in Islay, successively Colonel, Brigadier-General, and Major-General in the Revolutionary War, and later Delegate to the Continental Congress in 1780 and 1784, was described by Washington as "a brave soldier and distinguished patriot." Before the outbreak of the war he was a successful merchant, a leader of the "Sons of Liberty," and was the first American imprisoned for his utterances in behalf of independence. Macdougal Street, New York city, commemorates his name. Robert Erskine (1735-1780), geographer and Chief of Engineers on the staff of Washington, was a son of Rev. Ralph Erskine of Dunfermline. Washington erected a stone over his grave at Ringwood, New Jersey. Henry Knox (1750-1806), General of Artillery and Secretary of War (1785-95). Lieutenant-Colonel Richard Clough Anderson (1750-1826) was grandson of a Scottish emigrant. General James Ewing (c. 1736-1806), of Ulster Scot descent, served in Braddock's campaign and also during the Revolution. General William Wirt Henry was descended from an Ulster Scot who came between 1718 and 1722 to Massachusetts. General Richard Montgomery (1736-75), a descendant of the Montgomeries of Ayrshire, was killed while leading the attack on Quebec; and Major John Macpherson (1754-75), of Scots parentage, killed beside Montgomery, was the first soldier of prominence from Pennsylvania to be killed in the war. Bancroft calls him "the pure-minded, youthful enthusiast for liberty." Colonel Allan McLane (1746-1829), of Scottish origin, repeatedly referred to in Dr. Weir Mitchell's "Hugh Wynne," was one of the "Rough Riders" who patrolled the country around Philadelphia to prevent provisions reaching the British troops in the city. His flight and escape from the British in one of these raids was the subject of a painting by James Peale. General Hugh Mercer (c. 1725-1777), born in Aberdeen, died of wounds received at the battle of Princeton, also served with distinction in the Braddock and Forbes campaigns in western Pennsylvania. His life was a strenuous one, full of exacting and unselfish work for others, and as Judge Goolrick says in his "Life of Mercer," he "is entitled to the gratiude of all liberty-loving America." Mercer county, New Jersey, was named in his honor.

John Armstrong (1725-95), born in the North of Ireland of Scottish ancestry, served in the French and Indian War (1755-56), was Brigadier-General in the Continental Army (1776-77), and Delegate to the Continental Congress (1778-80, 1787-88). Colonel James Livingston (1747-1832), by his timely shot drove the British warship "Vulture" from her anchorage in the North River "thus securing the capture of André, effecting the discomfiture of Arnold's treason, and assuring the safety of West Point, the key of the Revolution." James Chrystie (1750-1807), born in or near Edinburgh, joined the Revolutionary Army and served with high reputation till the end of the war. On the discovery of Arnold's plot at West Point he was entrusted with a delicate mission by Washington, which he executed successfully. His son, Lieutenant-Colonel James Chrystie, earned a name for himself at the Battle of Queenstown in the war of 1812. William Davidson (1746-1781), born in Pennsylvania of Scottish parentage or descent, was a Brigadier-General in the Revolutionary Army, and was killed in the fight at the ford over Catawba River, January 31, 1781. Congress voted five hundred dollars for a monument to his memory, and Davidson College, North Carolina, is named in his honor. General William Macpherson (1756-1813), born in Philadelphia of Scottish parents, was in the British service at the time of the Revolution, but resigned and joined the colonies, and served faithfully under Washington. Major Robert Kirkwood was killed in the battle against the Miami Indians in 1792, the thirty-third time he had risked his life for his country. Lachlan McIntosh (1727-1806), of the family of MacIntosh of Borlum, was born in Badenoch, Inverness-shire, and came to America with his father who settled in Georgia. He volunteered his services on the outbreak of the Revolution, becoming General in 1776. He was second in command at Savannah and took part in the defence of Charleston. McIntosh county, Georgia, is named after his family, "whose members have illustrated the state, in both field and forum, since the days of Oglethorpe." William Moultrie (1731-1805), born in England or South Carolina, son of the Scottish physician, Dr. John Moultrie, ancestor of the Moultries of South Carolina, repulsed the attack on Sullivan's Island in 1776 and defended Charleston in 1779. Fort Moultrie was named in his honor. Andrew Pickens (1739-1817), of Scottish parentage, was noted as a partizan commander in South Carolina (1779-81), served with distinction at Cowpens in 1781, and captured Atlanta, Georgia, in the same year. Pickens county, Georgia, bears his name. John Stark (1728-1822), one of the most noted Generals of the Revolution, serving with distinction in several campaigns, was a member of the Court Martial which condemned Major André. Arthur St. Clair (1734-1818), born at Thurso,

Caithness, took part in many battles of the Revolution, was President of Congress in 1787, and Governor of the Northwest Territory (1789-1802). William Alexander (1726-83), titular Lord Stirling, born in Albany of Scottish parentage, commanded a Brigade at the Battle of Long Island, and also served at Trenton, Brandywine, Germantown, and Monmouth. John Paterson (1744-1808), grandson of a Dumfriesshire emigrant, took part in many battles of the Revolution, commissioned Major-General in 1783, the youngest one of that rank in the army, and was one of the organizers of the Society of Cincinnati. General Daniel Stewart was another patriot of the Revolution. A county in Georgia is named in his honor.

MEXICAN WAR. Winfield Scott (1786-1866), grandson of a Scot who fought at Culloden, was born in Virginia, and entered the army in 1808. He served with great ability in the War of 1812, later became Major-General and Commander-in-chief of the Army in 1841. During the war with Mexico he held chief command of the Army, and became Lieutenant-General in 1847. John Munroe (c. 1796-1861), born in Ross-shire, entered the United States Army, saw service against the Florida Indians, became Chief of Artillery under General Zachary Taylor in the Mexican War, and was subsequently Military and Civil Governor of New Mexico (1849-50). James Bowie (1795-1836), of Scottish descent and of "Bowie-knife" celebrity, took part in the Texan Revolution and was killed at the Alamo in 1836. Bowie county and the town of Bowie in Montague county, Texas, perpetuate his name. The Bowies were a prominent family in Maryland, occupying high positions in politics, jurisprudence, and society.

CIVIL WAR. General David Bell Birney (1825-64), son of James Gillespie Birney, served with distinction in the Army of the Potomac. General Ambrose Everett Burnside (1824-81), later Governor of Rhode Island (1867-69), and United States Senator (1875-81), was grandson of a Scot who emigrated to South Carolina at end of the eighteenth century. Samuel Wylie Crawford (1829-92), of Scottish ancestry, was brevetted Major-General of Volunteers for conspicuous gallantry, and wrote "Genesis of the Civil War" 1887). Major-General Thomas Ewing (1829-96), was descendant of Thomas Ewing who emigrated to New Jersey in 1715. James Lorraine Geddes (1829-87), born in Edinburgh, brevetted Brigadier-General for his services, was also a poet, and wrote "The Soldier's Battle Prayer," "The Stars and Stripes," etc. John Brown Gordon (1832-1904), Lieutenant-General in the Confederate Army and later Governor of Georgia, was descendant of John George Gordon and his wife Mary Chapman, emigrants from Scotland. General Charles Smith Hamilton (1822-96), of Scottish descent, also served with distinction in the

Mexican War. General Grant ascribed the success of the repulse at Corinth to him. Thomas Jonathan Jackson (1824-63), "Stonewall Jackson," the noted Confederate General, was of Ulster Scot descent. John Alexander Logan (1826-86), of Ulster Scot parentage, was later unsuccessful candidate for the Vice-Presidency in 1884, United States Senator (1871-77, 1879-86), and author of "The Great Conflict" (1866). Major-General Robert McAllister (1813-91), great-grandson of Archibald McAllister from Scotland, 1732. Charles Lafayette McArthur (1824-98), soldier, politician, and journalist, was of Scots parentage. General Arthur McArthur (1845-1912), of Scots parentage, son of Arthur McArthur the Jurist, later served in the Philippines, became in 1906 Lieutenant-General, being the twelfth officer in the history of the Army to attain that rank. Described as "our best read and best informed soldier." His son, Douglas, served with distinction in the Great War. John McArthur, born in Erskine, Scotland, in 1826, emigrated to United States in 1849, was brevetted Major-General for gallantry. General George Archibald McCall (1802-68), served in the Florida and Mexican Wars, and also rendered distinguished service in the Civil War. Daniel Craig McCallum (1815-78), born in Renfrewshire, Superintendent of the Erie Railroad (1855-56), was Director of Military Roads in the United States (1862-65), and became Major-General in 1866. "He introduced the inflexible arched truss, which has probably been in more general use in the United States than any other system of timber bridges." The McCooks, of Scottish descent, two Ohio families with a remarkable military record, often distinguished as the "Tribe of Dan" and "Tribe of John" from their respective heads—two brothers, Major Daniel and Dr. John McCook. All the sons, fourteen in number, served either in the Army or Navy, and all but one were commanding officers. Clinton Dugald McDougal (b. 1839), Major-General and later Member of Congress (1872-77), was born in Scotland. Irvin McDowell (1818-85), served in the Mexican War, in the Civil War had command of the Army of the Potomac, Major-General in 1872, was descendant of emigrant from Londonderry shortly after the siege in which his ancestor took part. General John Bankhead Magruder (1810-71) and Commander George Magruder of the Confederate Army were said to be "direct descendants of the illustrious Rob Roy McGregor." Alexander Mackenzie (b. 1844), Chief of Engineers, was of Scots parentage. David McMurtrie Gregg (b. 1833), served with distinction in battles of the Wilderness, and was afterwards Auditor-General of Pennsylvania. John McNeil (1813-91), Brigadier-General, was born in Halifax, Nova Scotia, of Scots parentage. General James Birdseye Macpherson (1828-64), of Ulster Scot descent, took a most prominent part in many battles. General Grant said at his death: "The country has lost one of its best soldiers, and I have lost my best friend. " William Macrae (1834-82), of Scottish descent, Brigadier-General in the Confederate Army was afterwards General Superintendent of the Wilmington and Manchester Railroad. William Addison Phillips (1824-93), soldier, statesman, and author, born in Paisley, refused to leave his command to accept the nomination for Governor of his state (Kansas). He was author of "Labor, Land, and Law" (1886). John Robertson (1814-87), born in Banffshire, was Adjutant-General of Michigan from 1861 to 1887. He was author of "The Flags of Michigan," "Michigan in the War," etc. James Alexander Walker (1832-1901), descendant of John Walker who came from Wigtown (c. 1730), was also Member of Congress (1895-99) and Lieutenant Governor of Virginia (1877).

SCOTS IN THE NAVY

John Paul Jones (1747-92), perhaps the most famous Scottish name in the annals of the American Navy, was the son of a Scottish gardener, and was born at Kirkbean, Kirkcudbrightshire. The details of his naval career are so well known that there is little use of repeating them here. James Craig (1735-1800), a Scot, was appointed by Congress a Commissioner of naval stores in 1776. He was owner of a number of armed privateering vessels, took several prizes, and also aided in fitting out several other vessels as privateers. The Nicholson family, of Scottish parentage, was famous in the naval annals of the United States for three generations, from the Revolution to the Civil War. Alexander Murray (1755-1821), grandson of a Scot, took an active part in the naval battles of the Revolution and commanded a squadron against the Barbary pirates in 1820. John Rodgers (1771-1838), of Scottish parentage, had a distinguished part in the war against Tripoli, the government of which he compelled to sign a treaty abolishing slavery of Christians and the levying of tribute on European powers. In the war of 1812 he fired the first gun, June 23, 1812, at the British frigate "Belvidere." He was afterwards offered, but declined, the office of Secretary of the Navy. George Campbell Read (c. 1788-1862), Admiral, of Ulster Scot descent, took part in the fight between the "Constitution" and "Guerrière" in 1812. Isaac McKeever (1794-1856), Commodore and Commandant of the Navy Yard as Portsmouth, Virginia, was of Scottish parentage. John Berrien Montgomery (1794-1873), descended from William Montgomery of Bridgend, Ayrshire (1701), served in the War of 1812, the Mexican War, and while too old for active service in the Civil War, was in charge of Boston Navy Yard, then one of the most important supply stations of the navy. Rear Admiral Andrew Bryson (1822-1892), of Scottish descent, took part in Civil War, and retired after forty-three years' continuous service. John McIntosh Kell (1823-1900), Executive Officer of the Confederate Cruiser "Alabama" and author of "Cruise and Combats of the 'Alabama'" was of Scottish origin. Rear Admiral Alexander Colden Rhind (1821-97), who served in the Mexican and Civil Wars, was also of Scottish descent. William Penn McCann (1830-1906), a descendant of John McKeand, a native of Whithorn, Wigtownshire, who settled here before the Revolution, was called "Father of the White Squadron" from his having the warships painted white. Francis Munroe Ramsay (1835-1914), Rear Admiral and Chief of the Bureau of Navigation (1889), Member of the Court of Inquiry which investigated the conduct of Rear Admiral Schley during the war with Spain, was a grandson of Patrick Ramsay who came from Scotland, c. 1750. Frederick Vallete McNair (1839-1900), Superintendent of the Naval Academy at Annapolis, was descended from Samuel McNair (1732). Rear Admiral George Wallace Melville (1841-1912), who saw considerable service in the Civil War and later achieved world wide fame as an Arctic explorer, was the grandson of a Scot from Stirling; and Admiral John Donaldson Ford (1840-1917), who fought in the Civil War and took a prominent part in the capture of Manila and destruction of the batteries at Cavite during the Spanish-American War, was of Scottish parentage.

SCOTS AS SCIENTISTS

Alexander Wilson (1766-1813), born in Paisley, the first naturalist to study American birds in their native haunts, and author of "American Ornithology" (1803-13), was also distinguished as a poet. David Hosack (1769-1835), one of the most distinguished surgeons and scientists of his day, fourth President of the New York Historical Society, was son of a native of Morayshire. Samuel Guthrie (1782-1848), physician and chemist, was descendant of John Guthrie, who came to America in 1661. He was one of the pioneers who introduced vaccination, produced the first successful percussion powder (after many experiments), invented the "punch lock" which superseded the flint-lock musket, and, in 1831, discovered the anæsthetic chloroform. Hugh Williamson (1735-1819), statesman and scientist, born in Pennsylvania and educated in Edinburgh. He studied theology and was licensed but never preached, was Professor of Mathematics in the College of Philadelphia (1760-63), studied medicine in Edinburgh and Utrecht, practised successfully, served as surgeon in the Revolutionary War, delegate to the Convention that framed the Constitution of the United States (1787), and was afterwards Member of the first Congress. John McLean (1771-1814), born in Glasgow, became Professor of Chemistry in Princeton (1775) and later Professor of Natural Philosophy and Chemistry in William and Mary College, Williamsburg, Virginia. His son, John, became President of Princeton. Dr. William Watson (d. 1828), a Scot, was physician and friend of Chancellor Livingston, and one of the early promoters of scientific agriculture in America. He was founder of the Farmers' Club of Dutchess and Columbia Counties, the pioneer of Agricultural Societies in New York. James Renwick (1790-1862), born in Liverpool of Scottish parents, was Professor of Physics in Columbia University, author of several scientific works, and one of the Commissioners who laid out the early boundary line of the Province of New Brunswick. His mother was the Jeannie Jaffray of several of Burns's poems. James Renwick, the architect, was his son. Other gifted sons were Edward Sabine Renwick and Henry Brevoort Renwick. Joseph Henry (1797-1878), the "Nestor of American Science," and organizer of the American Academy of Sciences otherwise the Smithsonian Institution in Washington, was of Scottish origin. His pa-

67

ternal and maternal grandparents emigrated from Scotland together and are said to have landed the day before the Battle of Bunker Hill. The McAllisters of Philadelphia (father and son) were famous as makers of optical and mathematical instruments, and the son was the first to study and fit astigmatic lenses, and was also the introducer of the system of numbering buildings according to the numbers of the streets, assigning one hundred numbers to each block. Spencer Fullerton Baird (1823-87), Naturalist and Secretary of the Smithsonian Institution, was also of Scottish origin. His works, including scientific papers, number over one thousand titles. Carlile Pollock Patterson (1816-81) did much to develop the United States Coast Survey. William Paterson Turnbull (1830-71), ornithologist, author of the "Birds of East Pennsylvania and New Jersey," a model of patient and accurate research, was born at Fala, near Edinburgh. Edward Duncan Montgomery, biologist and philosopher, was born in Edinburgh in 1835. Marshall MacDonald (1835-95), ichthyologist, pisciculturist, and inventor, engineer in charge of the siege of Vicksburg during the Civil War, and inventor of automatic hatching jars, was the grandson of a Scottish immigrant. Peter Smith Michie (1839-1901), soldier and scientist, born in Brechin, Forfarshire, graduated from West Point in 1863, served as Engineer in the Federal Army, and was afterwards Professor of Natural and Experimental Philosophy at West Point. William Healey Dall (b. 1845), palæontologist to the United States Geological Survey, author of "Alaska and Its Resources," and author of hundreds of articles on Natural History subjects, was a grandson of William Dall of Forfarshire. Thomas Harrison Montgomery (1873-1912), specialist in zoology and embryology, was of Scottish origin. Robert Gibson Eccles, physician and chemist, born in Kilmaurs, Ayrshire, in 1848, discovered that benzoic acid and the benzoates are excellent preservatives of food. He has been Chemist of the Department of Indian Affairs, Professor of Chemistry in the New York School of Social Economics, President of the New York Pharmaceutical Association, etc., and has written largely on philosophy and science. Stephen Alfred Forbes (b. 1844), naturalist, educator, and writer on entomology and zoology, is of Scottish origin. Thomas Craig (1853-1900), Mathematician and Editor of the American Journal of Mathematics, was of Scottish parentage. Alexander Crombie Humphreys, born in Edinburgh in 1851, became President of Stevens Institute of Technology, Hoboken, in 1902. Anstruther Davidson, born in Caithness in 1860, Associate Professor of Dermatology in the University of Southern California, is also distinguished as a botanist and entomologist.

William Maclure (1763-1840), the "Father of American Geology," was born in Ayr, Scotland, and after acquiring a fortune in London, he came in 1796 to the United States. Having studied geology in Europe he was attracted by the imposing scale of the geological structure of his adopted country, and in the course of some years made many journeys across the eastern states. He recorded his geological observations on a map, and in 1809 communicated his researches to the American Philosophical Society. In 1817, having extended his knowledge during the intervening eight years he presented his map to the Society, and it was then published. This was the first geological survey of the United States, and it was carried out unsustained by government aid or patronage. It was also chiefly through Maclure's aid that the new Academy of Sciences in Philadelphia was built and endowed. Dr. Archibald Bruce (1777-1818), the first scientific mineralogist in America, and founder of the *American Mineralogical Magazine* (1810), was born in New York city, son of Dr. William Bruce, head of the medical department of the British Armies. Henry Darwin Rogers (1808-66), born in Philadelphia of Ulster Scot parentage, Professor of Geology and Mineralogy in the University of Pennsylvania, State Geologist of Pennsylvania, published important works on the geology of Pennsylvania and New Jersey. He removed to Edinburgh in 1855 and three years later became Professor of Natural History in the University of Glasgow. His elder brother, William Barton Rogers (1804-1882), was also a distinguished physicist and geologist. David Dale Owen (1807-60), born in Lanarkshire, was brought to the United States by his father in 1823. In 1848 he took charge of the Geological Survey of Wisconsin and Iowa, and that of Minnesota in 1852. His brother, Richard Owen (1810-90), also born in Lanarkshire, had a distinguished career in this country as a geologist. J. Peter Lesley (1819-1903), also of Scottish descent, was another distinguished geologist who by his researches and surveys in Pennsylvania, vastly aided in the econômic development of that state. Persifor Frazer (1844-1909), son of John Fries Frazer and great-grandson of Lieutenant-Colonel Persifor Frazer of Revolutionary times, was author of the Geological Survey of Pennsylvania (5 vols.) William John McGee (1853-1912), geologist and anthropologist, claimed descent from the MacGregors. He was Geologist of the United States Geological Survey from 1883 to 1893, Ethnologist in Charge of the Bureau of Ethnology from 1893 to 1903, and in 1907 was appointed a Member of the Inland Waterways Commission. Washington Carruthers Kerr (1827-85), educator and scientist of Ulster Scot parentage, was State Geologist of North Carolina (1866-82), and published many papers and reports on his subject. John Muir (1838-1914), geologist, explorer, naturalist, and author, was born in Dunbar. "No man since Thoreau ever had keener sympathy with nature, a quicker vision for her mysteries, or a surer speech for their interpretation." The establishment of the Yosemite and Sequoia National Parks and the great Sierra Forest Reservation are due to his writings. The famous Muir Glacier in Alaska, discovered by him in 1879, will forever blazon his name. Other distinguished geologists who may be briefly mentioned are: Samuel Calvin (1840-1911), Professor of Geology in the University of Iowa, born in Wigtownshire; John James Stevenson (b. 1841), educator and geologist, of Scottish parentage; Erwin Hinckly Barbour (b. 1856), professor of Geology in the University of Nebraska; and William Berryman Scott (b. 1858), the distinguished geologist and palaeontologist of Princeton University.

Asa Gray (1810-88), the greatest of American botanists, was a descendant of one of the Ulster Scot settlers of 1718. Dr. Alexander Garden (1728-92), famous as a physician and botanist, was Professor of Botany in King's College (now Columbia University). His son was a distinguished Revolutionary officer. Thomas Huston Macbride (b. 1848), President Emeritus of the State University of Iowa, who has written much of value on botany, is of Scottish ancestry. Beverly Thomas Galloway (b. 1863), descended from John Galloway, an emigrant from Scotland in 1680, Chief of the Division of Plant Industry of the United States Department of Agriculture, Assistant Secretary of Agriculture in 1913-14, is the author of several works on plant diseases. David Trembly Macdougal (b. 1865), Director of the Botanical Research Department of the Carnegie Institution of Washington since 1905, is the grandson of a Scottish immigrant. His studies relate especially to plant physiology, heredity, and organic evolution.

Stephen Alexander (1806-83), son of a native of Scotland, wrote much on astronomy, and was chief of the expedition to the coast of Labrador to observe the solar eclipse in August, 1869. James Ferguson (1797-1867), an Engineer employed on the construction of the Erie Canal, was born in Perthshire. He was later Assistant Astronomer at the United States Naval Observatory, and discovered three asteroids, for which he received medals from the French Academy of Sciences. Ormsby McKnight Mitchel (1810-62), who was Director of the Cincinnati Observatory (1845) and later of the Dudley Observatory (1859), inventor of the chronograph and other astronomical apparatus, and became a General in the Civil War, was probably also of Scottish origin. Maria Mitchell (1818-89), daughter of William Mitchell (1791-1868), also an astronomer, became Professor of Astronomy in Vassar College, LL.D. of Columbia University (1887), and was the first woman elected to the American

Academy of Sciences. Lewis Morris Rutherfurd (1816-92), one of the most distinguished astronomers on the American Continent, obtained important results in astronomical photography, and by means of a ruling engine, designed by him in 1870, constructed the finest diffraction-gratings which had, up to that time, been made, was of Scottish ancestry. George Davidson (1825-1911), born in England of Scottish parentage, geodetist and astronomer, one of the founders of the Geographical Society of the Pacific, Regent of the University of California, was retired after fifty years' active field service of incalculable value to the cause of science. William Harkness (1837-1903), born in Ecclefechan, Dumfriesshire, was executive officer of the Transit of Venus Commission (1882). The task of reducing the observations and the hundreds of photographs was successfully undertaken by him although declared impossible by eminent British and German astronomers. He was later Astronomical Director of the Naval Observatory and in 1897 made head of the Nautical Almanac. Williamina (Mina) Paton Fleming (1857-1911), born in Dundee, discovered many new stars and wrote much of permanent value on her subject. William Wallace Campbell (b. 1862), of Scottish ancestry, has been Director of Lick Observatory since 1901, and has written much on astronomy.

The most interesting Scot in connection with horticulture in the United States is Grant Thorburn (1773-1861), who was born in Dalkeith and left his native country for political reasons in 1794. After trying a number of occupations he finally established himself as a seed merchant in New York, and the business is still carried on under his name. Under the pen name of "Lawrie Todd" he contributed to the *Knickerbocker Magazine* and other New York periodicals. and supplied John Galt, the novelist, with much of the information incorporated in his "Lawrie Todd; or, Settlers in the New World." Thorburn also pubished two volumes of reminiscences, "Forty Years' Residence in America," and "Fifty Years' Reminiscences of New York." William Adair, born near Glasgow in 1815, developed a profitable business as gardener and horticulturist in Michigan, and served as State Senator from 1861 to 1865, 1869-70. Peter Henderson (1822-90), born at Pathhead near Edinburgh, founded the firm of Peter Henderson and Co., horticulturists and seedsmen, one of the largest firms of its kind in existence. William Saunders (1822-1900), born in St. Andrews, planted and laid out several large estates, beautified Fairmount and Hunting Parks in Philadelphia, and the park and garden system of Washington, D. C., the National Cemetery at Gettysburg, etc. William Macmillan, born in Nairnshire, laid out the public parks of Buffalo, and William R. Smith, a native of Haddingtonshire, was for many years Superintendent of the Botanic Gardens at Washington. Robert Buist (1805-80), born in Edinburgh, was also one of the greatest horticulturists in the United States.

SCOTS AS PHYSICIANS

A prominent physician of early colonial times was Dr. Gustavus Brown (1689-1765), born in Dalkeith, and died in Maryland. Dr. Gustavus Richard Brown (1747-1804), born in Maryland and educated at Edinburgh University, his son, also made a reputation for himself as a physician of ability. Dr. Gustavus Brown (1744-1801), grandson of the first named, was summoned to attend President Washington in his last illness. Dr. John Lining (1708-1760), born in Scotland, settled in Charleston, S. C., in 1730, gained a large practice through his skill as a physician, and a distinguished reputation in Europe as a scientist from his experiments in electricity, etc. His meteorological observations were probably the first ever published. In 1751 he issued his "History of the Yellow Fever," "which was the first that had been given to the public from the American continent." Dr. Lionel Chalmers (1715-1777), born in Argyllshire, practised in South Carolina for more than forty years, and was the first to treat of the soil, climate, weather, and diseases of that state. He "left behind him the name of a skilful, humane physician." Dr. James Craik (1731-1814), physician-general of the United States Army, was born at Arbigland, near Dumfries, and for nearly forty years was the intimate friend of Washington, and his physician in his last illness. One of the earliest introducers of vaccination into America and an original investigator into the cause of disease was Dr. John Crawford (1746-1813), of Ulster Scots birth. As early as 1790 he had conceived what is now known as the germ theory of disease. Dr. Adam Stephen, born in Scotland, died at Martinsburg, West Virginia, in 1791, took part in the French and Indian wars and was an active participant in the Revolutionary War on the side of the colonists. The town of Martinsburg in Berkeley County was laid out by him. Dr. George Buchanan (1763-1808), founder of the Medical and Chirurgical Faculty of Maryland, was a grandson of George Buchanan, the Scot who laid out Baltimore town in 1730. Dr. John Spence (1766-1829), born in Scotland, educated at Edinburgh University, settled in Virginia in 1791, and obtained a high reputation as a judicious and successful practitioner. The "father of ovariotomy," Dr. Ephraim McDowell (1771-1830), was born in Virginia of Scots ancestry and studied medicine at the University of Edinburgh. James

Brown McCaw (1772-1846), one of the leading surgeons in Virginia for over thirty years, studied medicine in Edinburgh. He was one of the first, if not the first, to tie the external carotid artery, an operation he performed in 1807. He came of a race of doctors, being the great-grandson of James McCaw, a surgeon who emigrated from Wigtownshire in 1771. George McClellan (1796-1847) the eminent surgeon and founder of the Jefferson Medical College at Philadelphia, was of Scottish descent. His son, John Hill Brinton McClellan (1823-74), was professor of anatomy in Pennsylvania Medical College, and his grandson was George McClellan (1849-1913), the eminent Philadelphia anatomist. Dr. Peter Middleton (d. 1781), a native of Scotland, made the first dissection on record in this country before a class of students and in 1767 established a Medical School in New York which was subsequently merged in the King's (now Columbia) College. Dr. William Currie (1754-1823), served in the medical service during the Revolutionary War, and was reputed one of the most gifted men of his time as physician and classical scholar. Horatio Gates Jameson (1778-1855), distinguished physician and surgeon, was son of Dr. David Jameson who had emigrated to Charleston in 1740 in company with Dr. (afterwards General) Hugh Mercer. Granville Sharp Pattison (1791-1851), anatomist, born near Glasgow, held several professional appointments in this country and founded the Medical Department of the University of the City of New York. Dr. John Kearsley Mitchell (1793-1858), poet, botanist, and eminent physician of Philadelphia, was son of Dr. Alexander Mitchell who came from Scotland in 1786. His son, Dr. Silas Weir Mitchell, born in 1829, was distinguished for his researches in toxicology, the nervous system, etc., and as one of the most distinguished of American authors. One of the founders of the City Hospital, Albany, and Surgeon-General of New York State, was Dr. James McNaughton (1796-1874), born at Kenmore, Aberfeldy. Dr. Daniel McRuer (1802-73), born in Knapdale, Argyllshire, "a typical Scotchman with a 'burr' in his talk," performed great service in the Civil War as an army Surgeon. Dr. John Watson (1807-1863), organizer of one of the first dispensaries for the treatment of skin diseases and introducer of reforms in the New York Hospital, was an Ulster Scot. John Murray Carnochan (1817-87), one of the most distinguished surgeons of his day, was of Scottish parentage. Ferdinand Campbell Stuart (b. 1815), inventor of various instruments used in genito-urinary diseases and one of the founders of the New York Academy of Medicine, was grandson of Rev. Archibald Campbell of Argyllshire. Dr. David Hayes Agnew (1818-92) was of Scottish descent. In his work "he attained a degree of eminence which has rarely, if ever, been equaled, and to which our own times and generation furnish no parallel." William Thomas Green Morton (1819-68), the discoverer of anæsthesia, was also of Scottish origin. Dr. Robert Alexander Kinloch (1826-91), of Scottish parentage, was the first American surgeon to resect the knee joint for chronic cases, also the first to treat fractures of the lower jaw and other bones by wiring the fragments, and was also the first in any country to perform a laparotomy for gunshot wounds in the abdomen without protrusion of the viscera. Dr. George Troup Maxwell (1827-1879), was inventor of the laryngoscope. James Ridley Taylor (1821-1895), who entered the medical profession after middle life, at the end of a long career passed as a mechanical engineer, and achieved success and fame in his profession, was born in Ayr, Scotland. He probably inherited his mechanical skill from his uncle, John Taylor of Dalswinton, who constructed the steam engine along with Symington. James Henry McLean (1829-86), physician and Member of Congress, was born in Scotland. Dr. James Craig (1834-88), obstetrician, born in Glasgow, graduated at the University of the City of New York, attended over four thousand cases without the loss of a mother, was inventor of several surgical appliances, and was the first to demonstrate hydriodic acid as a curative in acute inflammatory rheumatism. Professor Alexander Johnson Chalmers Skene (1837-1900), of Brooklyn, born in Fyvie, Aberdeenshire, was perhaps the most famous Gynecologist in America. He was author of many treatises on his special subject. Prof. Charles McBurney (b. 1845), the famous surgeon, was of Scottish ancestry. Neil Jamieson Hepburn, born in Orkney in 1846, oculist and aurist, held many positions of responsibility. Charles Smith Turnbull (.b. 1847), oculist and eminent specialist in diseases of the ear, was of Scottish parentage. Alexander Hugh Ferguson (1853-1911), the famous Chicago surgeon of Scottish parentage, was decorated by the King of Portugal for his skill in surgery. Other prominent doctors and surgeons of Scottish origin whom we have only space to name are: John Barclay Crawford (1828-94); William Smith Forbes (1831-1905), grandson of Dr. David Forbes of Edinburgh; John Minson Galt (d. 1808), and his son Alexander D. Galt (1777-1841); Robert Ramsey Livingston (1827-88), the most prominent of Nebraska's early physicians; and James Macdonald (1803-49), resident physician of Bloomingdale Asylum.

SCOTS IN EDUCATION

The Scots have largely contributed to raise the standard of education and culture in the United States. They furnished most of the principal schoolmasters in the Revolutionary Colonies south of New York, and many of the Revolutionary léaders were trained by them. While Harvard still continued under the charge of a president and tutors and had but one "professor," William and Mary College had had for many years a full faculty of professors, graduates of the Scottish and English universities. The Scots established the "Log College" at Nashaminy, Pennsylvania, Jefferson College, Mercer College, Wabash College, and Dickinson College; and in many places, before the cabins disappeared from the roadside and the stumps from the fields, a college was founded. The "Log College" was the seed from which Princeton College sprang. The University for North Carolina, founded and nurtured by Scots in 1793, and the University of Pennsylvania and Princeton University are indebted to the same source for their present position. William Gordon and Thomas Gordon, who founded a free school in the county of Middlesex, Virginia, in the latter half of the seventeenth century, were Scots; and Hugh Campbell, another Scot, an Attorney-at-law in Norfolk county, Virginia, in 1691, deeded two hundred acres of land in each of the counties of Norfolk, Isle of Wight, and Nansemond, for free schools. James Innes, who came to America from Canisbay, Caithness, in 1734, by his will gave his plantation, a considerable personal estate, his library, and one hundred pounds "for the use of a free school for the benefit of the youth of North Carolina," the first private bequest for education in the state. One of the first public acts of Gabriel Johnston, Provincial Governor of North Carolina (1734-52), was to insist upon the need of making adequate provision for a thorough school system in the colony. Out of the host of names which present themselves in this field of public service we have room only for the following:

James Blair (1656-1743), born in Edinburgh, was the chief founder and first President of William and Mary College, and Mungo Inglis was the first Grammar Master there till 1712. Francis Alison (1705-99), an Ulster Scot educated in Glasgow, was Vice-Provost of the College of Philadelphia, now the University of Pennsylvania. David

Rhind, tutor of John Rutledge, "an excellent classical scholar, and one of the most successful of the early instructors of youth in Carolina," was of Scottish birth. The tutor of Thomas Jefferson was also a Scot. Samuel Finley (1715-66), born in Armagh of Scots ancestry, S.T.D. of Glasgow University, 1763, was President of the College of New Jersey, and one of the ancestors of Samuel Finley Breese Morse, inventor of the Morse system of telegraphy. In educational work in the eighteenth century no name stands higher than that of William Smith (1727-1803), born in Aberdeen, first Provost of the College of Philadelphia. He was the introducer of the system of class records now used in all American universities. Isabella Graham (1742-1814), born in Lanarkshire, ranked as one of the most successful teachers in New York at the end of the eighteenth century. James Dunlap (1744-1818), of Scottish descent, was President of Jefferson College, Pennsylvania. William Graham (1745-99), was first President of Washington College (now Washington and Lee University). Robert Patterson (1743-1824), a Scot of Ulster, was Vice-Provost of the University of Pennsylvania (1810-13), and Director of the United States Mint in Philadelphia (1805-24). His son, Robert M. Patterson, succeeded him as Vice-Provost in 1828. Peter Wilson (1746-1825), born at Ordiquhill, Aberdeenshire, published several important text-books on Latin and Greek, was Member of the New Jersey Legislature in 1777, and in 1783 was appointed to revise and codify the laws of the state of New York. Thomas Craighead (1750-1825), first President of Davidson Academy (1785-1809), afterwards the University of Nashville, was great-grandson of Rev. Robert Craighead who went from Scotland to Donoghmore in Ireland. Joseph McKeen (1757-1807), first President of Bowdoin College, was of Ulster Scot origin (1718). John Kemp (1763-1812), born at Auchlossan, Aberdeenshire, became Professor of Mathematics in Columbia University. He "had an important influence in moulding the views of De Witt Clinton on topics of internal improvement and national policy." John Brown (1763-1842), Professor of Logic and Moral Philosophy in the University of South Carolina, was afterwards third President of the University of Georgia. Joseph Caldwell (1773-1835) was Founder and President of the University of North Carolina. Jesse Mercer (1769-1841), Founder of Mercer University, was the grandson of a Scottish emigrant to Virginia. Robert Finley (1772-1817), Trustee of the College of New Jersey (1807-17) and fourth President of the University of Georgia, was of Scottish parentage. John Mitchell Mason (1770-1829), fourth President of Dickinson College and for several years Foreign Secretary of the American Bible Society, was the son of Dr. John Mason, born in Linlithgow. Both were ministers of the

Associate Church in New York. Archibald Alexander (1772-1851), fourth President of Hampden-Sidney College, Virginia (1796-1806), and Professor in Princeton Theological Seminary (1812-51), was of Scottish parentage. James Waddell Alexander (1804-59), Professor of Rhetoric and Belles-Lettres at Princeton (1833-44) and of Ecclesiastical History and Church Government in Princeton Theological Seminary (1844-51) was his son. Joseph Addison Alexander (1809-60), Orientalist and Biblical critic, was another son of Archibald Alexander. Moses Waddell (1770-1840), born in Iredell county, North Carolina, of Scottish parentage, fifth President of the University of Georgia, was one of the foremost teachers of his day. Samuel Brown Wylie (1773-1852), Vice-Provost of the University of Pennsylvania (1834-45), was born in Antrim of Scottish parents and educated in Glasgow. Joseph McKean (1776-1818), Boyleston Professor of Rhetoric in Harvard University (1809-18) was of Scottish parentage. Charles Macalister (1798-1873), born in Philadelphia of Scottish parentage, intimate friend of five Presidents, Government Director of the United States Bank, was founder of Macalister College, Minneapolis. John Dempster (1794-1863), President of the Illinois Wesleyan University, was of Scottish parentage. Daniel Curry (1809-87) was President of De Pauw University (1855-59). Andrew Harvie, born in Scotland before 1810, became Principal of the Tecumseh branch of the State University of Michigan (1839-40), Master of Chancery (1848), State Senator (1850-51). Described as a "man of ability and thorough culture." Nathaniel Macon Crawford (1811-71), fourth President of Mercer University and afterwards President of Georgetown College, Kentucky, was a son of William H. Crawford the statesman. John Forsyth (1811-86), clergyman, author, and Professor of Latin in Rutgers College, was of Scottish parentage, and received his education in Edinburgh and Glasgow. James McCosh (1811-94), born at Carskeoch, Ayrshire, was President of Princeton University from 1868 to 1888, and was the author of many works on philosophy. John Fries Frazer (1812-72), Vice-Provost of the University of Pennsylvania (1858-68), was of Scottish ancestry. Louis Agassiz described him as "the first of American physicists of his time." James Sidney Rollins (1812-88), of Ulster Scot origin, for his efforts on behalf of education in his state was declared by the Curators of the University of Missouri to have won the honorable title of "Pater Universitatis Missouriensis." Daniel Kirkwood (1814-95), mathematician and educator, grandson of Robert Kirkwood who came from Scotland c. 1731, was Professor of Mathematics at Indiana University (1856-86). David Chassel, "of Scotch descent and Scotch characteristics," was tutor to Professor James Hadley, America's greatest Greek scholar. Joshua Hall McIlvaine (1815-97), a distinguished compartaive philologist, was President of Evelyn College, Princeton. Alexander Melville Bell (1819-1905), the "Nestor of elocutionary science," inventor of the method of phonetic notation of "visible speech," was born in Edinburgh. Alexander Martin (1822-93), sixth President of De Pauw University, was born in Nairn, Scotland. John Fraser (c. 1823-1878), second Chancellor of the University of Arkansas, was born in Cromarty, Scotland. Malcolm Mac-Vicar, born in Argyllshire in 1829, was famous as an educator, writer of text-books, and inventor of many devices to illustrate principles in arithmetic, astronomy and geography. John Maclean (1798-1886), tenth President of Princeton University, was of Scottish parentage. Matthew Henry Buckham (b. 1832), eleventh President of the University of Vermont, was born in England of Scottish parentage. James Kennedy Patterson (b. 1833), first President of the Agricultural and Mechanical College of Kentucky (1880-1901), was born in Glasgow. David French Boyd (1834-99), second President of Louisiana State University, and his brother, Thomas Duckett Boyd, also a University President, were descended from John Boyd of Ayrshire, who emigrated to Maryland in 1633. William Henry Scott (b. 1840), third President of Ohio State University and Professor of Philosophy there, was of Scottish ancestry. Neil Gilmour, born in Paisley, Scotland, in 1840, was Superintendent of Public Instruction of New York State; and James MacAlister (1840-1913), born in Glasgow, was the first Superintendent of Schools in Philadelphia, where he introduced many reforms, notably in the Kindergarten and in co-ordination of teaching. In 1891 he became President of the Drexel Institute and was also author of several works on education. Thomas Davidson (1840-1900), philosopher, educator, and author, was born at Deer, Aberdeenshire. John McLaren McBride (b. 1846), of Scottish parentage, was President of the University of South Carolina. Gustavus Richard Glenn (b. 1848) descended from Nicholas Glenn, an emigrant from Scotland, filled several important educational positions and was afterwards President of North Georgia Agricultural College. George Edwin Maclean (b. 1850), a distinguished English and Anglo-Saxon scholar, was fifth Chancellor of the University of Nebraska. William Milligan Sloan (b. 1850), author, educator, and Professor of History in Columbia University, is descended from William Sloane, a native of Ayr, who settled here in the beginning of the nineteenth century. James Cameron Mackenzie (b. 1852), born in Aberdeen, is founder of the Mackenzie School for Boys at Dobbs Ferry (1901) and a frequent contributor to educational publications. James Hervey Hyslop (b. 1854), philosopher, psychologist, and educator, was grandson of George Hyslop of Roxburghshire. He devoted many years to psychical research. James Geddes (b. 1858), philologist and Professor of Romance Languages in Boston University, is of Scottish parentage. Andrew Armstrong Kincannon (1859-1917), Chancellor of the University of Missisippi, was descendant of James Kincannon who came from Scotland c. 1720. Edwin Boone Craighead (b. 1861), Professor of Greek at Wofford College, South Carolina, and afterwards third President of Tulane University, is of Scottish descent. John Huston Finley (b. 1863), President of the College of the City of New York and New York State Commissioner of Education, is a descendant of a brother of Samuel Finley, President of Princeton College. Andrew Cunningham McLaughlin, born in 1861, Professor of American History in the University of Michigan, is the son of a Peebles lawyer. Duncan Black Macdonald, Professor of Semitic Languages at Hartford Theological Seminary, was born in Glasgow in 1863. Richard Cockburn Maclaurin (1870-1920), seventh President of Massachusetts Institute of Technology, was born in Lindean, Selkirkshire. George Hutcheson Denny (b. 1870), Professor of Latin in Washington and Lee University, and later President of the same institution, and James Gray McAllister (b. 1872), sixteenth President of Hampden-Sidney College, are both of Scottish descent. William Allan Neilson, born in Doune, Perthshire, was Professor of English in Harvard University (1906-17), and is now President of Smith College, Northampton, Massachusetts. William Douglas Mackenzie, President of Hartford Theological Seminary Foundation, is a son of John Mackenzie of Knockando, Morayshire, and was born in Fauresmith, South Africa, in 1859.

As librarians may legitimately be included under the head of educators, the following individuals may be mentioned: John Forbes (1771-1824), born in Scotland, was Librarian of the New York Society Library. His son, Philip Jones Forbes (1807-77), was Librarian of the same institution from 1828 to 1855, and his son, John born in 1846, afterwards became Librarian there. Morris Robeson Hamilton (b. 1820), State Librarian of New Jersey, was descendant of John Hamilton, acting Governor of New Jersey (d. 1746). John Cochrane Wilson (1828-1905), Librarian of the Law Library of the Equitable Life Assurance Company. Miss Catherine Wolf Bruce established a Free Circulating Library in Forty-second Street in memory of her father, George Bruce the typefounder, in 1888. It is now a branch of the New York Public Library.

SCOTS IN LITERATURE

John Lawson (c. 1658-1711), Surveyor-General of North Carolina, a native of Aberdeen, published "A New Voyage to Carolina," in 1709, reprinted 1714, 1718, 1737, 1860, and twice translated into German (1712, 1722). Lawson was cruelly murdered by the Tuscaroras. Hugh Henry Brackenridge (1748-1816), born near Campbeltown, Argyllshire, Judge of the Supreme Court of Pennsylvaina, was author of a political satire, "Modern Chivalry," a work now extremely rare. David Ramsay (1749-1815), physician and patriot, of Ulster Scot descent, Delegate to the Continental Congress, was author of historical works relating to the Revolution and to South Carolina. Gilbert Imlay, born about 1755 in New Jersey of Scottish parents, was the first Kentucky novelist, author of "The History of an Expatriated Family" (1793), etc. Robert Dinsmoor (1757-1836), poet, was brother of Governor Dinsmoor of New Hampshire. Hugh McCall (1767-1824), author of the first "History of Georgia," (published in 2 v., 1811-16), was of Scottish descent. His ancestor emigrated from Dumbartonshire to Ulster along with the ancestor of J. C. Calhoun. The ancestors of both remained two generations in Ulster before coming to America. The greatest name in American literature is that of the son of the Orcadian farmer, Washington Irving (1783-1859). He was the first who won international honors for American literature. John Mellish or Melish (1771-1822), born in Perthshire, died in Philadelphia, traveled extensively in the United States and published several volumes of his travels and also published many topographical and military maps. James Murdock (1776-1856), of Ulster Scot descent, translated and edited Mosheim's "Institutes of Ecclesiastical History," Milman's "History of Christianity," etc. Henry Marie Brackenridge (1786-1871), author and jurist, was son of the author of "Modern Chivalry." Thomas F. Gordon (1789-1860), lawyer and historian of New Jersey, Pennsylvania, etc., was of Scottish ancestry. Augustus Baldwin Longstreet (1790-1870), lawyer, newspaper editor, author of "Georgia Scenes" (1840), etc., was son of the inventor. Lydia (Huntley) Sigourney (1791-1865), poet and miscellaneous writer, was partly of Scots descent. Hew Ainslie (1792-1878), author of a "Pilgrimage to the Land of Burns," etc., was born in Ayrshire. David Paul Brown (1795-1872), born in Philadelphia of

Scottish parents, was author of "The Forum; or Forty Years of Practice at the Philadelphia Bar." James Lawson (1799-1880), newspaper editor and dramatist, was born in Glasgow and died in Yonkers. Angus Umphraville of Missouri, the unknown author of "Missourian Lays" (St. Louis, 1821), was most probably a Scot. His verses are described as "simply wonderful." Maria J. McIntosh (1803-78), authoress, was descended from the McIntoshes of Georgia. George Washington Bethune (1805-62) of New York, a graceful poet and eloquent orator, was the son of Divie Bethune, a native of Dingwall. Robert Shelton Mackenzie (1808-80), born in Dublin of Scottish parentage, was editor of the standard edition of "Noctes Ambrosianæ," and in 1834 became the first regular salaried correspondent of an American newspaper, the New York "Evening Star." Rev. Robert Turnbull (1809-77), born at Whitburn, Linlithgowshire, edited the "Christian Review" for many years and was author of several works. James C. Moffat (1811-90), orientalist, poet, and Professor of Classics in Lafayette College, author of "Comparative History of Religions," etc., was born in Glencree, Wigtownshire. Robert Macfarlane (1812-83), Editor of the "Scientific American," and author of two or three technical treatises, was born in Rutherglen. John Milton Mackie (1813-94), of Scottish ancestry, was author of several important biographical works. William Scoular (1814-72), born in Kilbarchan, Editor of the Lowell "Courier" (1841-47), published the "History of Massachusetts in the Civil War" (1868-71). Arthur MacArthur (1815-96), Jurist and Lieutenant Governor of Wisconsin (1856-58), born in Glasgow, was author of "Education in Relation to Manual Industry" (1884) and "Biography of the English Language" (1889). William Ross Wallace (1819-81), author of "Perdita," etc., was described by Bryant as "a born poet." Donald Macleod (1821-65), son of the Rev. Alexander Macleod of Mull, Professor of Rhetoric in Mount St. Mary's College, Ohio, was author of historical and other works. His brother, Xavier Donald Macleod, was a poet and miscellaneous writer. Donald Grant Mitchell (1822-1908), "Ik Marvel," was of Scottish descent, and so was General Lew Wallace (1827-1905), author of "Ben Hur," etc. James Grant Wilson (1832-1914), son of the poet publisher, William Wilson, of Poughkeepsie, was born in Edinburgh, and attained the rank of General in the Civil War. He was afterwards author of several important biographical and historical works. William Swinton (1833-92), journalist, was correspondent of New York "Times" (1862-64), and author, was born in Haddingtonshire. He "produced many educational works which were widely adopted in both private and public schools throughout the country." Henry Ward Beecher called him the "American Napier" from the vividness of his historical descriptions. David Gray (1836-88), editor of the Buffalo "Courier" and poet, was born in Edinburgh. John Clark Ridpath (1841-1900), educator, historian, and author, was decended from the old Border family of Redpath. He was the author of "Great Races of Mankind" (1893), "History of the World" (1898), etc. Katherine Margaret Brownlee (b. 1841), a descendant of the Brownlees of Torwood, was author of several volumes of poetry. Leonard Allison Morrison (b. 1843) of New Hampshire, was a descendant of John Morrison who went from Scotland to Londonderry and thence to Londonderry, New Hampshire, in 1723. Always devoted to literary studies, as a historical and genealogical writer he has earned an enviable reputation. James Morrison Steele Mackaye (1842-94), actor and dramatist, was grandson of William Kay who came from Scotland about 1800. His son, Percy Wallace Mackaye (b. 1875) is a distinguished dramatist and poet. Wallace Bruce (b. 1844), poet and essayist, w s descended from George Bruce who came from Scotland in 1635. While United States Consul at Edinburgh (1889-93) he secured the erection of a statue of Lincoln in the Calton Burial Ground, to commemorate the services of Scottish-American soldiers in the Civil War. James Kennedy, born at Aberlemno, Forfarshire, in 1850, is a well-known poet, author, and lecturer. John D. Ross, born in Edinburgh in 1853, is author of several literary works particularly relating to Scotland. Francis Marion Crawford (1854-1909), the novelist, son of Thomas Crawford the sculptor, was also of Scottish descent. Henry Morse Stephens, the historian, was born in Edinburgh in 1857. Ernest Evan Seton-Thompson (b. 1860), artist, author, and naturalist, and Charles William Wallace (b. 1865), philologist and Shakespearean scholar, are both of Scottish descent. John Hanson Thomas McPherson (b. 1865), historian and educator, author of "History of Liberia" (1891), is a descendant of Robert McPherson who came from Scotland in 1738. George Barr McCutcheon (b. 1866), author of many widely read works of fiction ("Graustark," "Brewster's Millions," etc.) is a descendant of John McCutcheon who emigrated from Scotland in 1730. Mary Johnston (b. 1870), author of "Prisoners of Hope" (1898), "To have and to hold" (1899), etc., is a descendant of Peter Johnston who emigrated to Virginia in 1727.

SCOTS IN THE CHURCH AND SOCIAL WELFARE

Francis Makemie (c. 1658-1708), the organizer of the first American Presbytery, was born in Ulster of Scots parentage. In 1676 he went to Glasgow to attend the classes in the University there, and his name still stands in the matriculation register of the University: "Franciscus Makemius . . . Scoto-Hibernus," i. e. Francis Makemie, a Scot of Ireland. In 1683 he was ordained by the Presbytery of Laggan and sent over to the American colonies, where he immediately began the organization of churches and presbyteries. William Traill, another Scot, Moderator of the Presbytery of Laggan, was sent over shortly before Makemie but he confined his work to preaching. George Gillespie (1683-1760), born in Glasgow, was one of the earliest ordained ministers in New Jersey and Delaware. Alexander Garden (1685-1756), an Episcopalian, born in Edinburgh, settled in Charleston, South Carolina, as Rector of St. Philip's Episcopal Church. Samuel Auchmuty (1722-77), son of the eminent Scottish lawyer of Boston, was Rector of Trinity Church, New York city, and had charge of all the churches there. Thomas Gordon, the "fighting parson" of Bacon's Rebellion (1676) was a Scot. Henry Barclay (1712-64), Rector of Trinity Church, New York, Trustee of the New York Society Library, and a Governor of Columbia University, was the son of John Barclay, a Scot, Surveyor General of East New Jersey. Robert Sandeman (1718-71), born in Perth, and died in Danbury, Connecticut, was principal founder of the Sandemanians or Glassites. John Mason, a native of Linlithgow, "one of the most accomplished preachers and pastors of his day," was appointed Minister of the Scotch Presbyterian Church, New York, in 1761. James Caldwell (1734-81), soldier parson of the Revolution, was of Scots parentage or descent. Finding the Revolutionary soldiers short of wadding he distributed the church hymn books among them, with the exhortation, "Now, boys, put Watts into them." His son, John E. Caldwell, was one of the founders of the American Bible Society. Alexander McWhorter (1734-1807), of Scottish parentage, took an active part in Revolutionary matters and was a Trustee of Princeton College. McWhorter Street in Newark, New Jersey, is named in his honor. James Waddell (1739-1805), famous in Virginia as "The Blind Preacher," was probably a grandson or great-grandson of William Waddell of Monkland parish, Scotland, one of the prisoners captured at Bothwell

Brig in 1679. Samuel McClintock (1732-1804), minister of Greenland, New Hampshire, of Scottish origin, was present at Bunker Hill and appears in Trumbull's painting of the battle. Four of his sons served in the Revolutionary war. Alexander McLeod (1774-1833), born in the island of Mull, died in New York as Pastor of the First Reformed Church. Described as "a powerful preacher, a man of learning and wisdom, and a devout Christian." George Buist (1770-1808), born in Fifeshire, Scotland, educated in Edinburgh, "one of the most eloquent and distinguished divines of his day," was Pastor of the Scots Church in Charleston and President of the College of Charleston. Alexander Campbell (1786-1866), founder of the Campbellites, was born in Antrim of Scots ancestry. Walter Scott, another of the founders, was born in Moffat, Dumfriesshire. John Dempster (1794-1843), founder of Boston Theological Seminary, which afterwards became the Theological School of Boston University, was of Scots parentage. Peter Douglas Gorrie (1813-84), clergyman, and historian of the Methodist Church in the United States, was born in Glasgow. John McClintock (1814-70), of Drew Theological Seminary and leading editor of McClintock and Strong's "Cyclopædia of Biblical, Theological, and Ecclesiastical Literature," was of Scottish descent. Robert Stuart MacArthur, born in Canada, in 1841, of Scots parentage, Minister of Calvary Baptist Church, New York, has published many volumes of sermons, essays, and narratives of travel. Robert Mackenzie (b. 1845), President of San Francisco Theological Seminary, was born in Cromarty. Robert McIntyre (b. 1851), Methodist Episcopal Bishop of California, was born in Selkirk. Joseph Plumb Cochran, Medical Missionary to Persia, the "Hakim Sahib" of the natives, was grandson of a Scot. John Alexander Dowie (1848-1907), founder of the so-called "Christian Catholic Apostolic Church in Zion," was born in Edinburgh. Mary M. Baker Glover Eddy (1821-1910), claimed partly Scots descent (from MacNeils of Barra).

Charles Pettigrew (1743-1807), Bishop of the Diocese of North Carolina, was of Scottish descent. James Kemp (1764-1827), second Bishop of Maryland, was born at Keithhall in Aberdeenshire. Charles Pettit McIlvaine (1799-1873), Bishop of Ohio (1832-73), author of "Evidences of Christianity," 1832, was also of Scottish origin, from the MacIlvaines of Ayrshire. William Edward McLaren (1831-1905), third Bishop of Chicago, was grandson of a Scot. The first missionary Bishop of Duluth, James Dow Morrison (b. 1844), was son of Rev. John Morrison and his wife who emigrated from Glasgow in 1837. Abram Newkirk Littlejohn (1824-91), first Bishop of Long Island, was a descendant of Hugh Littlejohn of Perthshire.

James Steptoe Johnston (b. 1843), second Bishop of western Texas, was of Scottish descent; and Hugh Miller Thompson (1830-1902), second Bishop of Mississippi, was an Ulster Scot, born in Londonderry. Richard Gilmour (1824-91), second Roman Catholic Bishop of the Diocese of Cleveland (1872-91), born in Glasgow, Scotland, of Presbyterian parents, was noted for his zeal in behalf of Catholic education. Robert Seton (b. 1839), a descendent of the Setons of Winton, was created Archbishop of Heliopolis in 1903. Elizabeth Ann Bayley Seton (1774-1821), of the same family, was founder of the Roman Catholic Order of Sisters of Charity (1809), of which she was the first Mother Superior.

John McLean (1759-1823), merchant and philanthropist, was founder of McLean Asylum for Insane at Somerville, Massachusetts. Robert Rantoul (1778-1848), of Scottish parentage, worked hard to ameliorate the criminal legislation of the country, and took part in establishing a charity school at Beverly, Massachusetts, which was said to be the first Sunday School in America. Mrs. Graham, a Scotswoman, celebrated in New York city for her benevolence and charity, founded a Sunday School in New York for young women in 1792. The movement however languished for some years until her daughter, Mrs. Bethune, also born in Scotland, organized the Female Sabbath School Union of New York in 1816. By her work in this connection Mrs. Bethune earned her title of "Mother of Sabbath Schools in America." Fanny Wright (1795-1852), Madame Frances D'Arusmont, born in Dundee, Scotland, lectured extensively in the United States on social, religious, and political questions, and was the author of "Views on Society and Manners in America," etc. Robert Dale Owen (1801-77), born in Glasgow, social reformer, spiritualist, author, and Member of Congress from Indiana (1843-47), was a strong advocate of negro emancipation. James Miller McKim (1810-1874), of Ulster Scot descent, was one of the organizers of the National Anti-Slavery Society (1835), later publishing agent of the Pennsylvania Anti-Slavery Society, and in 1865 one of the founders of the New York "Nation." Albert Brisbane (1809-90), of Scottish and English descent, was the "Father of American Fourierism." Albert Keith Smiley (1828-1912), educator and reformer, was born in Maine of Scottish ancestry; and Thomas Kirby Cree, of Ulster Scot origin, was Secretary for twenty-five years of the International Committee of the Young Mens' Christian Association. John MacVicar born in Canada in 1859 of Scottish parents, was one of the originators of the Commission form of government, developing what became known as the "Des Moines Plan." James Duncan, born in Kincardine in 1857, is the well-known Labor Leader.

SCOTS AS LAWYERS

John Mercer (1704-68), author of "An exact abridgment of all the public Acts of Assembly," Williamsburg, 1737, was a descendant of the Mercers of Aldie. Robert Auchmuty (born in Scotland, died in Boston, 1750), and his sons were distinguished lawyers of Colonial times. Hugh Maxwell (1787-1873), born in Paisley, was Assistant Judge Advocate General (1814) and District Attorney of New York (1819-29). Edward Duffield Ingraham (1793-1854), of Scottish descent, was at the head of the legal profession of his time in Philadelphia. He was also an eminent bibliophile, possessing a library of thirty thousand volumes. Robert Rantoul (1805-52), of Scots ancestry, was member of the first Commission to Revise the Laws of Massachusetts, Member of the first Massachusetts Board of Edcation, "an honor intended to be conferred only on such as were well qualified by their literary acquisitions to discharge its responsible duties." He was also a prominent agitator against the fugitive slave law, and organizer and corporator of the Illinois Central Railroad, the first transcontinental line projected. John Jay McGilvra (1827-1903), of Scots parentage, took part in many prominent enterprises for the public benefit in Washington State, and forced the Northern Pacific Railroad to restore five million acres to public domain. Lawrence Maxwell, born in Glasgow in 1853, was Solicitor-General of the United States (1893-95), and also held many other important positions. David Robert Barclay, author of the well known "Barclay's Digest" of the decisions of the Supreme Court (St. Louis, 1868) was of Scots descent. William Birch Rankine (1858-1905) of Scots parentage, took up the work of developing Niagara power and founded the Niagara Falls Power Company (1886). Thomas M. Logan (b. 1840), lawyer, soldier, and railroad officer was a descendant of Logan of Restalrig. David Clarence Gibboney (b. 1869), Special Counsel for the Pure Food Commission in 1906, grandson of a Scot, has also made a reputation for prosecution of gamblers, dive-keepers, illicit liquor dealers, etc., in Philadelphia.

SCOTS IN ART, ARCHITECTURE, ETC.

John Smibert (c. 1684-1751), born in Edinburgh, came to America in 1728 and settled in Boston, where he met success as a portrait painter. He was the first painter of merit in the colonies, and painted portraits of many of the eminent magistrates and divines of New England and New York between 1725 and 1751, the year of his death. His work had much influence on the American artist, John Singleton Copley. Gilbert Charles Stuart (1755-1828), born in Rhode Island of Scottish parents, was the foremost American portrait painter of his day. He painted several portraits of Washington, and also portraits of Presidents John Adams, John Quincy Adams, Jefferson, Madison, Justice Story, Fisher Ames, John Jacob Astor and others. Cosmo Alexander, a skilled portrait painter, born in Scotland, was his teacher for a time. Charles Fraser (1782-1860), born in Charleston, South Carolina, of Scottish ancestry, first studied law and retired with a competency. He then took up art and achieved eminent success in miniature painting and as a painter of landscapes, pictures of genre, still life, etc. William Dunlap (1766-1839), artist and dramatist, founder and early Vice-President of the National Academy of Design, was of Ulster Scot descent. His family name was originally Dunlop. Robert Walter Weir (1803-89), of Scots parentage, is best known for his historical pictures, he being one of the first in America to take up this branch of the art. "The Embarkation of the Pilgrims" (1836-40) in the Rotunda of the Capitol at Washington is by him. Russell Smith, born in Glasgow in 1812, was a scientific draughtsman and landscape painter. Two of his finest landscapes, "Chocorua Peak" and "Cave at Chelton Hills" were exhibited in the Philadelphia Exhibition of 1876. His son, Xanthus (b. 1839), was a well-known marine and landscape painter and painted many of the naval engagements of the Civil War. James Hope, born near Abbotsford in 1818, settled in New York in 1853, distinguished as a landscapist, was chosen an Associate of the National Academy in 1865. Alexander Hay Ritchie (1822-95), born in Glasgow and educated in Edinburgh, was a most successful painter in oils as well as an engraver in stipple and mezzotint. His paintings of the "Death of Lincoln" and "Washington and his Generals," obtained great popularity. As a portrait painter fine examples of his work are "Dr. McCosh" of Princeton, "Henry

Clay," etc. He also did a good deal of book illustrating. Thomas Lachlan Smith (d. 1884), also born in Glasgow, was noted for his Winter scenes. Two notable pictures of his, "The Deserted House" and "The Eve of St. Agnes," were exhibited at the Centennial Exhibition. Still another Glasgow artist, John Williamson (1826-85), born at the Tollcross in that famous city, became an Associate of the National Academy, and made the scenery of the Hudson and the Catskills his special study as shown by his "The Palisades," "Sugar Loaf Mountain," "Autumn in the Adirondacks," etc. William Hart (1823-94), born in Paisley, became an Academican in 1857, and was afterwards President of the Brooklyn Academy and of the American Water Color Society. James McDougall Hart (1828-1901), born in Kilmarnock, brother of William Hart, already mentioned, Academican of the National Academy of Design, was noted for his landscapes and paintings of cattle and sheep. His "Summer Memory of Berkshire" and his "Indian Summer" attracted considerable attention at the Paris Salon in 1878. James David Smillie (1833-1909), son of James Smillie, the Scottish engraver, during the Civil War made designs for government bonds and greenbacks. In 1864 he took up landscape painting and was one of the founders of the American Water Color Society (1867) and National Academican in 1876. His brother, George Henry Smillie (b. 1840), was also distinguished as a landscape painter. He made a sketching tour in the Rocky Mountains and the Yosemite Valley in 1871, and became a National Academican in 1882. Walter Shirlaw, born in Paisley, Scotland, in 1838, died in Madrid, Spain, in 1909, was the first President of the Society of American Artists. His easel pictures "are marked by rich color and fine composition, and he is one of the few American artists who have successfully painted the nude. His water-colors and etchings have brought him high reputation in these forms of expression." Walter MacEwen, born in Chicago of Scottish parents, has painted many pictures and has received medals and decorations for his work. In 1895-96 he painted nine large panels and a number of small ones for the Hall of Heroes in the Library of Congress. George Inness (1825-94), the famous American painter, is believed to have been of Scottish ancestry. James T. Dick (1834-68), William Keith (b. Aberdeenshire, 1839), Robert Frank Dallas (b. 1855), John White Alexander (b. 1856), Robert Bruce Crane (b. 1857), Addison Thomas Miller (b. 1860), and John Humpreys Johnston, are all artists of Scottish parentage or Scottish ancestry. John Robinson Tait (b. 1834), artist and author, son of a native of Edinburgh, has written much on art subjects. John Wesley Beatty (b. 1851), Art Director of the Carnegie Institute, Pittsburgh, is of Scottish parentage. John Ward

Dunsmore (b. 1856), Director of the Detroit Museum of Arts and Founder of the Detroit School of Arts; and John Ferguson Weir (b. 1841), Dean of the School of Fine Arts at Yale University, are of Scottish descent.

Alexander Lawson (1773-1846), born in Lanarkshire, died in Philadelphia, was famous as the engraver of the best plates in Alexander Wilsons's *Ornithology* and the plates on conchology for Haldeman and Binney. His son, Oscar A. Lawson (1813-54), was chart 'engraver of the United States Coast Survey, 1840-51. Samuel Allerdice engraved a large number of plates of Dobson's edition of Rees's *Cyclopædia*, 1794-1803. Hugh Anderson, a Scot, did good line and stipple work in Philadelphia in the first quarter of the nineteenth century. George Murray, born in Scotland, died in Philadelphia in 1822, organized the bank-note and engraving firm of Murray, Draper, Fairman & Co., in 1810-11, the best note engravers in this country in their day. John Vallance, also born in Scotland, died in Philadelphia in 1823, was one of the founders of the Association of Artists in America, and Treasurer of the Society of Artists in Philadelphia in 1810. James Smillie (1807-85), born in Edinburgh, died in New York, was celebrated as an engraver of bank notes and as an engraver of landscapes. Among his best works are Cole's series "The Voyage of Life," and Bierstadt's "Rocky Mountains." Dr. Alexander Anderson (1775-1870), the "Bewick of America," born in New York of Scots parentage, at the age of ninety-three engraved some illustrations for Barbour's "Historical Collections of New Jersey." Robert Hinschelwood, born in Edinburgh in 1812, studied under Sir William Allen, was landscape engraver for Harpers and other New York publishers and also engraver for the Continental Bank Note Company. John Geikie Wellstood, born in Edinburgh in 1813, was another eminent engraver. In 1858 his firm was merged in the American Bank Note Co., and in 1871 he founded the Columbian Bank Note Company of Washington, D. C. He also made many improvements in the manufacture of banknotes. Charles Burt (c. 1823-92), born in Edinburgh, died in Brooklyn, a pupil of William Home Lizars of Edinburgh, did some fine plates and portraits for books and for several years was one of the chief engravers for the Treasury Department in Washington. Hezekiah Wright Smith, born in Edinburgh, in 1828, engraved portraits of Daniel Webster, Edward Everett, and his head of Washington, after the Athenæum head by Gilbert Stuart, is said to be "the best engraving of this famous portrait ever made." Nathaniel Orr (b. 1822), of Scottish ancestry, retired in 1888 "with the reputation of having brought the art of wood engraving to the highest perfection, and the signature 'Orr,' cut in the block was always a sure guarantee of art excellence." Robert Shaw, born in Delaware in 1859 of Scottish parentage, has made a reputation by his etchings of famous historical buildings. His etching, the "Old Barley Mill" ranks as one of the best etchings made in this country. A few other Scottish engravers who produced good work were Robert Campbell, William Charles (d. Philadelphia, 1820), Alexander L. Dick (1805), W. H. Dougal (he dropped the "Mac" for some reason), Helen E. Lawson (daughter of Alexander Lawson already mentioned), John Roberts (1768-1803), William Main Smillie (1835-88), son of James Smillie mentioned above, and William Wellstood (1819-1900).

John Crookshanks King (1806-82), born in Kilwinning, Ayrshire, emigrated to America in 1829, and died in Boston, was celebrated for his busts of Daniel Webster, John Quincy Adams, Louis Agassiz, the naturalist, Ralph Waldo Emerson, etc. He also excelled as a maker of cameo portraits. Thomas Crawford (1814-57), one of the greatest if not the greatest sculptor of America, was of Scottish descent. His works include "Armed Liberty" (bronze doors), Beethoven, bust of John Quincy, Washington, "Orpheus," etc. Frederick William Mac-Monnies, born in Brooklyn in 1863 of Scottish parents (his father was a native of Whithorn, Wigtownshire), is sculptor of the statue of Nathan Hale in City Hall Park, New York; "Victory" at West Point, etc. Robert Ingersoll Aitken, born in San Francisco of Scottish parents, is designer of the monuments to President McKinley at St. Helena, Berkeley, and in Golden Gate Park, San Francisco. He also designed the monument to the American Navy in Union Square, San Francisco. In 1906 he moved to New York and has executed busts of some of the most prominent Americans of the day. Notable of his ideal sculptures are "Bacchante" (1908), "The Flame" (1909), and "Fragment" (1909). John Massey Rhind, Member of the National Sculpture Society, one of the foremost sculptors of the present day, was born in Edinburgh in 1858. James Wilson, Alexander Macdonald (1824-1908), and Hermon Atkins MacNeil (1866) are also of Scottish origin.

Alexander Milne Calder, born in Aberdeen, Scotland, in 1846, began life as a gardener, studied with Alexander Brodie and John Rhind and in London and Paris, came to America in 1868, and is best known as having made the sculpture for the Philadelphia City Hall including the heroic statue of William Penn, which crowns the tower. His son, Alexander Stirling Calder, born in Philadelphia in 1870, is also a sculptor of note, and was acting chief of the Department of Sculpture, Panama-Pacific Exposition, San Francisco, 1913-1915. Robert Tait MacKenzie, born in Ontario, Canada, in 1867, :··: of Rev. William Mackenzie, a graduate of Edinburgh, has created several groups of athletes in action of great force and beauty. Dr. Mackenzie is a physician and director of the Department of Physical Education in the University of Pennsylvania. Thomas MacBean, the architect of St. Paul's Chapel, Broadway, New York City, built in 1764-66, was a Scot who received his training under James Gibbs (an Aberdonian), architect of St. Martin-in-the-Fields, London. John Notman (1810-65), born in Edinburgh, designed and constructed some of the most important buildings in Philadelphia and also the State Capitol, Trenton. James Renwick (1818-95), born in New York city of Scottish ancestry, planned the distributing reservoir on Fifth Avenue, New York, where the New York Public Library now stands. He was one of the greatest architects in this country, and the beauty of his work—to cite only a few of his most notable creations—is amply attested by Grace Church, Calvary Church, and St. Patrick's Cathedral, in New York; the Smithsonian Institution and Corcoran Art Gallery, in Washington; and Vassar College in Poughkeepsie. John McArthur (1823-90), born in Bladenoch, Wigtownshire, designed and constructed Philadelphia City Hall, Lafayette College, the "Public Ledger" building in Philadelphia, several hospitals, etc. Alexander Campbell Bruce (b. 1835), of Scottish parentage, designed a number of court-houses and other public buildings in Tennessee, Georgia, Alabama, Florida, and North Carolina, besides schools, libraries, churches, hotels, etc. He easily became the foremost architect of the South. Henry Hobson Richardson (1838-86), of Scottish descent, drew the plans for many important buildings, but Trinity Protestant Episcopal Church in Boston, is considered his masterpiece. James Hamilton Windrim (b. 1840), architect and Director of Public Works in Philadelphia, was of Ulster Scot parentage. His services were utilized in the planning and construction of some of the most important buildings in Philadelphia. The Masonic Temple in that city is believed to be his masterpiece. The designer of many of the notable bridges of Philadelphia was Frank Burns (1844-1913), an architectural draughtsman of Scottish descent. Harold Van Buren Magonigle (b. 1867), designer of the monument to the Seamen of U. S. S. *Maine* (1900), Cornell Alumni Hall, Ithaca, the National McKinley Memorial at Canton, Ohio, etc., is the grandson of John Magonigle of Greenock. The builder of the world famed Smithsonian Institution in Washington was Gilbert Cameron (d. 1866), a native of Greenock, and Scottish stone-masons were largely employed in the construction of many of the most important buildings in the country, such as the Metropolitan Museum and Tombs in New York, the Capitol in Albany, the State House in Boston, the City Hall in Chicago, etc. Alexander McGaw (1831-1905), born in

Stranraer, Wigtownshire, was famous as a bridge-builder and as builder of the pedestal of the Statue of Liberty in New York Harbor. John L. Hamilton (1835-1904), born in Newmilns, Ayrshire, came to the United States in 1853, and soon became eminent as a builder. Duncan Phyfe, maker of exquisite furniture, who adapted and improved the Sheraton style, and considered by good judges to be the equal of Sheraton, Hipplewhite, and Adams, was a Scot who came to America about 1784. His father was John Fife of Inverness. Dyer, who devotes a chapter of his *Early American Craftsmen* to him, says "no other American made anything comparable to . . . the exquisite furniture of Duncan Phyfe." The name of Samuel McIntire (d. 1811) stands out pre-eminent as master of all the artists in wood of his time. An account of his work is given by Dyer with illustrations of his work. In 1812, Thomas Haig, a native of Scotland, a Queensware potter, started the Northern Liberties Pottery, and turned out a beautiful quality of red and black earthenware. About 1829 the works of the Jersey Porcelain and Earthenware Company (founded 1825) were purchased by David and J. Henderson. Some of the productions of the Hendersons are especially sought after by collectors. The firm is now known as the Jersey City Pottery. The Scottish firm of J. and G. H. Gibson, glass-stainers, Philadelphia, obtained a national reputation for artistic work. Daniel and Nathaniel Munroe, clockmakers, were famous as such in Massachusetts in the beginning of the nineteenth century. Henry Mitchell (1810-93), born in Fifeshire, was the pioneer wagon-builder of the west. Frederick Turnbull (1847-1909), who introduced the art of Turkey-red dyeing into this country about 1850, was born in Glasgow.

Will C. Macfarlane (b. 1870), organist and composer, was born in England of Scottish origin. His compositions include songs, anthems, organ music, a Lenten Cantata, "The Message from the Cross." His setting of Katherine Lee Bates's patriotic hymn, "America, the Beautiful," has had nation-wide usage. William Wallace Gilchrist (b. 1846), composer, was of Scottish descent; and Edward Alexander MacDowell (1861-1908), composer and Professor of Music in Columbia University, was of Ulster Scot origin.

Robert Campbell Maywood (1784-1856), actor and theatrical manager in Philadelphia, was born in Greenock, Scotland. Edwin Forrest (1806-1872), the celebrated American actor, was the son of a native of Dumfriesshire; and Robert Bruce Mantell, who made his debut in Rochdale, England, was born in Irvine, Ayrshire, in 1854. James Edward Murdoch (1811-93), grandson of a Scottish immigrant, was Professor of Elocution at Cincinnati College of Music, and later a leading actor on the American stage. During the Civil War he devoted his energies to support of the Union and gave readings for the benefit of the United States Sanitary Commission. Benjamin Franklin Keith (1846-1914), theater proprietor, was of Scottish descent. Mary Garden, Singer and Director of Grand Opera, was born in Aberdeen in 1877. James H. Stoddart, the veteran actor, was also of Scottish origin.

SCOTS AS INVENTORS

As Scotland gave to the world the knowledge of the art of logarithms, the steam engine, the electric telegraph, the wireless telegraph, illuminating gas, the knowledge of chloroform, and many other important inventions, it was to be expected that the inventive faculty of her sons would not fail when transplanted to this country.

Hugh Orr (1717-98), born in Lochwinnoch, inventor of a machine for dressing flax, took a patriotic part in the war of the Revolution by casting guns and shot for the Continental Army, besides doing much to encourage rope-making and spinning. His son, Robert, invented an improved method of making scythes and was the first manufacturer of iron shovels in New England. William Longstreet (1759-1814), a New Jersey Scot, invented and patented an improvement in cotton-gins called the "breast-roller," also a portable steam saw-mill. As early as 1790 he was at work on the problem of the application of steam power to the propulsion of boats, but lack of funds prevented operations until 1807, the same year in which Fulton launched his steamboat. His son, Augustus Baldwin Longstreet (1790-1870), became President of South Carolina College. Robert Fulton (1765-1815), of Ayrshire origin through Ulster, was, as every one knows, the first to successfully apply steam to navigation. Hugh Maxwell (1777-1860), publisher and newspaper editor, of Scottish descent, invented the "printer's roller" (patented in 1817), cast his own types and engraved his own woodcuts. Henry Burden (1791-1871), born in Dunblane, inventor of an improved plow and the first cultivator, was also the first to invent and make the hook-headed railroad spike "which has since proved itself a most important factor in railroad building in the United States." His "cigar boat" although not a commercial success was the fore-runner of the "whale-back" steamers now in use on the Great Lakes. William Orr (1808-91), manufacturer and inventor, born in Belfast of Ulster Scot parentage, was the first to manufacture merchantable printing paper with wood fibre in it, and made several other improvements and discoveries along similar lines. Cyrus Hall McCormick (1809-84), inventor of the reaping machine, was descended from James McCormick, one of the signers of the address of the city and garrison of Londonderry presented to William III. after the siege in 1689. Of his invention the

French Academy of Sciences declared that by its means he had "done more for the cause of agriculture than any other living man." James Blair (1804-84), born in Perth, Scotland, was the inventor of the roller for printing calico; and Robert M. Dalzell (1793-1873) was inventor of the "elevator system" in handling and storing grain. Samuel Colt (1814-62), inventor of the Colt revolver, and founder of the great arms factory at Hartford, Conn., was of Scots ancestry on both sides. He was also the first to lay a submarine electric cable (in 1843) connecting New York city with stations on Fire Island and Coney Island. Thomas Taylor, inventor of electric appliances for exploding powder in mining, blasting, etc., Chief of the Division of Microscopy (1871-95), was born in Perth, Scotland, in 1820. Duncan H. Campbell, born in Greenock in 1827, settled in Boston as a lad, by his numerous inventions, "pegging machines, stitching machines, a lockstitch machine for sewing uppers, a machine for using waxed threads, a machine for covering buttons with cloth," laid the foundation of New England's pre-eminence in shoe manufacturing. Gordon McKay (1821-1903), by his inventions along similar lines also helped to build up New England's great industry. Robert Dick, (1814-93), born in Bathgate, Linlithgowshire, died in Buffalo, lecturer, newspaper editor, writer, preacher, and inventor, was inventor of the mailing machine used in nearly every newspaper office on the continent. Alexander Morton, (1820-60), the perfector if not the inventor of gold pens, was born in Darvel, Ayrshire. James Oliver, born in Roxburgh, Scotland, in 1823, made several important discoveries in connection with casting and moulding iron, was the inventor of the Oliver chilled plow, and founder of the Oliver Chilled Plow Works, South Bend, Indiana. The business established by him is now carried on in several cities from Rochester, New York State, to San Francisco, and south to Dallas, Texas. William Chisholm, born in Lochgelly, Fifeshire, in 1825, demonstrated the practicability of making screws from Bessemer steel, organized the Union Steel Company of Cleveland, (1871), and devised several new methods and machinery for manufacturing steel shovels, scoops, etc. His brother, Henry, was the first to introduce steel-making into Cleveland, and might justly be called "The Father of Cleveland." Andrew Campbell (1821-90) was the inventor of many improvements in printing machinery, and of a long series of devices comprising labor-saving machinery relating to hat manufacture, steam-engines, machinists' tools, lithographic and printing machinery, and electrical appliances. William Ezra Ferguson (b. 1832), merchant and inventor of the means of conveying grain on steam shipments without shifting, was of Scottish ancestry. Alexander Davidson (b. 1832) made many inventions in connection with the typewriter, one of the most important being the scale regarding the value of the letters of the alphabet. As an inventor he was of the front rank. Andrew Smith Hallidie (b. 1836), son of a native of Dunfermline, was the inventor of steel-wire rope making and also the inventor of the "Hallidie ropeway," which led up to the introduction of cable railroads. James Lyall (1836-1901), born in Auchterarder, invented the positive-motion shuttle (1868) which revolutionized the manufacture of cotton goods. He also invented fabrics for pneumatic tyres and fire-hose. James P. Lee, born in Roxburghshire in 1837, was inventor of the Lee magazine gun which was adopted by the United States Navy in 1895. His first weapon was a breech-loading rifle which was adopted by the United States Government during the Civil War. Later he organized the Lee Arms Company of Connecticut. The production of the telephone as a practical and now universally employed method of "annihilating time and space" in the articulate intercourse of the human race will forever be associated with the name of Alexander Graham Bell, born in Edinburgh in 1847. By its means he has promoted commerce, created new industries; and has bridged continents, all the result of "sheer hard thinking aided by unbounded genius." To Dr. Graham Bell we are also indebted for the photophone, for the inductoin balance, the telephone probe, and the gramophone. During the war he designed a "submarine chaser" capable of traveling under water at a speed of over seventy miles an hour, and he has made important experiments in the field of aeronautics and in other arts and sciences. The mother of Thomas Alva Edison (b. 1847), it may here be mentioned, was of Scottish parentage (Elliott). The originator of the duplex system in the manufacture of railroad tickets was William Harrison Campbell (1846-1906), of Scottish parentage. William Malcolm (1823-90), also of Scottish parentage, was the inventor of telescopic sights, an invention adopted by all civilized governments. His attainments were better known and appreciated in Europe than in his own country. Daniel McFarlan Moore, electrician and inventor, of Ulster Scot descent, was inventor of the Moore electric light. James Peckover, born in England of Scottish and English ancestry, invented the saw for cutting stone and a machine for cutting mouldings in marble and granite. Rear-Admiral George W. Baird (b. 1843), naval engineer, invented the distiller for making fresh water from sea water, and patented many other inventions in connection with machinery and ship ventilation. James Bennett Forsyth (b. 1850), of Scottish parentage, took out more than fifty patents on machinery and manufacturing processes connected with rubber and fire-hose. John Charles Barclay, telegraph manager, descendant of John Barclay who emigrated from Scotland in 1684, patented the printing telegraph "said to be the most important invention in the telegraph world since Edison introduced the quadruplex system." Alexander Winton, born in Grangemouth in 1860, inventor and manufacturer, successfully developed a number of improvements in steam engines for ocean going vessels, founded the Winton Motor Carriage Company in 1897, and patented a number of inventions in connection with automobile mechanism. The works of the company at Cleveland, Ohio, now cover more than thirteen acres. The first to expound and formulate the application of the law of conservation in illumination calculations was Addams Stratton McAllister (b. 1875), a descendant of Hugh McAllister, who emigrated from Scotland c. 1732. He also holds several patents for alternating-current machinery, and has written largely on electrical subjects. Richard Dudgeon (1820-99), born in Haddingtonshire, Scotland, was distinguished as a machinist, inventor of the hydraulic jack and boiler-tube expander.

SCOTS AS ENGINEERS

Thomas. Hutchins (1730-1789), engineer and geographer was of Scotish origin. He was author of some topographical works and also furnished the maps and plates of Smith's Account of Bouquet's expedition (Philadelphia, 1765). James Geddes (1763-1838), of Scottish birth or parentage, was surveyor of canal routes in New York State and was chief engineer on construction of the Erie Canal (1816), and chief engineer of the Champlain Canal (1818. "In all matters relating to the laying out, designing and construction of canals, he was looked upon as one of the highest authorities in the country." James Pugh Kirkwood (1807-77), born in Edinburgh, came to United States in 1832, was one of the most eminent engineers in the country, one of the founders of the American Society of Civil Engineers (1852) and President (1867-68). James Laurie (1811-75), born at Bell's Mills, Edinburgh, Chief Engineer on the New Jersey Central Railroad, consulting engineer in connection with the Housatonic Tunnel, and first President of the American Society of Civil Engineers. William Tweeddale, born in Ayrshire in 1823, rendered valuable engineering service in the Civil War, and was an authority on the sources and character of water supply. Henry Brevoort Renwick, noted engineer and expert in patent cases, first inspector of steam vessels for the Port of New York, was a son of James Renwick the scientist. David Young, born in Alloa, Scotland, in 1849, was President of the Consolidated Traction Lines of New Jersey and General Manager of the larger consolidated company. William Barclay Parsons (b. 1859), is partly descended from Colonel Thomas Barclay, a Tory of the Revolution. Hunter McDonald (b. 1860), descended from Angus McDonald, a refugee from Culloden, is a prominent railroad engineer. T. Kennard Thomson, born in 1864, is prominent as a bridge builder, designer of pneumatic caissons, etc. His father came from Stranraer in 1834. Hugh Gordon Stott, born in Orkney, in 1866, President of the American Institute of Electrical Engineers (1907), Superintendent of motive power of Manhattan Railway System, etc. William Gibbs McNeill (1801-53), of Scottish parentage, was another engineer worth mentioning. Theodore Crosby Henry (1841-1914), "the father of irrigation in Colorado," was also of Scottish descent. William McLean (d. 1839), brother of Judge McLean, was mainly instrumental in extending the Ohio Canal from Cincinnati to Cleveland. John Findley Wallace (1852-1920), of Scottish descent, was chief-engineer of the Panama Canal (1904-05), and also designed and constructed many important engineering works. Angus Sinclair (1841-1919), born in Forfarshire, was an engineer, author of several textbooks on engineering, and editor of the "Railway and Locomotive Engineering."

SCOTS IN INDUSTRIES

Robert Gilmor (1748-1822), born in Paisley, was the founder of the East India trade in this country. He also assisted in founding the first bank in Baltimore (the Bank of Maryland), and the Maryland Historical Society. His son Robert (1774-1848) was also prominent in Baltimore business and was President of the Washington Monument Association which laid the foundation for the Washington monument in Baltimore in 1815 and completed it in 1829. Henry Eckford (1775-1832), shipbuilder, was a native of Irvine, Ayrshire. On the outbreak of the War of 1812 he built several ships for the American Government for use on the Great Lakes. In 1820 he was appointed Naval Constructor at the Brooklyn Navy Yard and there built six ships of the line. In 1822 he built the steamer "Robert Fulton," which made the first successful steam voyage to New Orleans and Havana. Angus Neilson Macpherson (1812-76), born at Cluny, Inverness-shire, was builder of the frigate "Ironsides," and designer of the furnaces for heating large plates and the method of affixing them to the sides of the vessel. Donald Mackay (1810-80), born in Nova Scotia, grandson of Donald Mackay of Tain, Ross-shire, established the shipyards at East Boston, and constructed a number of fast sailing ships, and during the Civil War a number of warships for the United States Government. The beauty and speed of his clippers gave him a world wide reputation as a naval constructor. Thomas Dickson (1822-84), President of the Delaware and Hudson Canal Co., was born in Lauder. William Grey Warden (1831-95), born in Pittsburgh of Scottish ancestry, was a pioneer in the refining of petroleum in Pennsylvania, and the controlling spirit in the work of creating the great Atlantic Refinery consolidated with the Standard Oil Company of Ohio in 1874. George Gibson McMurtry (1838-1915), born in Belfast of Scotttish descent, steel manufacturer and philanthropist, was "one of the big figures of that small group of men which established the industrial independence of the United States from the European nations of cheap labor." James Edwin Lindsay (1826-1919), lumberman, was descended from Donald Lindsay, who settled in Argyle, New York, in 1739. John McKesson (b. 1807), descended from the McKessons of Argyllshire, was founder of the wholesale drug firm of McKesson and Robbins; and Alfred B. Scott of the wholesale drug firm of Scott and Bowne was also of Scottish descent. Edmond Urquhart (b. 1834) was one of the pioneers in the creation of the cotton seed oil industry. To Andrew Carnegie (1835-1919), born in Dunfermline, "the richest and most free-handed Scot who ever lived," more than anyone else is due the great steel and iron industry of the United States. His innumerable gifts for public libraries, etc., are too well known to need detailing here. To New York alone he gave over five million dollars to establish circulating branches in connection with the New York Public Library. In the development of the steel business of Pittsburgh he was ably seconded by James Scott, George Lauder (his cousin), Robert Pitcairn, Charles Lockhart, and others—all Scots. James McClurg Guffey (b. 1839), oil producer and capitalist, was of Galloway descent. He developed the oil fields of Kansas, Texas, California, West Virginia, and Indian Territory. The town of Guffey, Colorado, is named in his honor. His brother Wesley S. Guffey was also prominent in the oil industry. John Arbuckle (1839-1912), merchant and philanthropist, known in the trade as the "Coffee King," was born in Scotland. Robert Dunlap (b. 1834), hat manufacturer and founder of Dunlap Cable News Company (1891), was of Ulster Scot origin. William Chalk Gouinlock (1844-1914), physician and manufacturer, of Scottish ancestry, was one of the first to establish the salt industry in Western New York (1883), and in 1887 established the first salt-pan west of the Mississippi (at Hutcheson, Kansas). Edward Kerr, born in Sanquhar, Dumfriesshire, in 1842, was founder of the Laurenceville Bronze Company (1891); and William Mackenzie (1841-1914), born in Glasgow, was founder of the Standard Bleachery at Carlton Hill, New Jersey. Hugh J. Chisholm (1847-1912), capitalist and manufacturer, was of Scottish parentage. James Smith Kirk (1818-86), soap manufacturer in Chicago, was born in Glasgow. George Yule, born in Rathen, Aberdeenshire, in 1824, was distinguished in manufactures. William Chapman Ralston (1826-75), developer of California, was of Scottish ancestry. William Barr (1827-1908), merchant and philanthropist, founder of one of the largest dry goods firms in the Middle West, was born in Lanark. Matthew Baird (1817-77), born in Londonderry of Ulster Scot parentage, a partner in the Baldwin Locomotive Works, in 1865 became sole proprietor besides being a director in several other important corporations. James Douglas Reid (1819-1901), born in Edinburgh, superintended the construction of many of the most important telegraph lines in the United States and founded and edited the "National Telegraph Review." Theodore Irwin (b. 1827), grain merchant, manufacturer, and bibliophile; and Edward Henry Kellogg

(b. 1828), manufacturer of lubricating oils, were of Scottish descent. James Abercrombie Burden (b. 1833), ironmaster and manufacturer, was son of the great Scottish inventor, Henry Burden. William Sloane (d. 1879), came to the United States in 1834 and established the great carpet firm of William Sloane and Sons. The development of the tobacco industry which so enriched Glasgow in the middle of the eighteenth century, drew large numbers of Scots to Virginia as merchants and manufacturers, and, says Slaughter, "it is worthy of note that Scotch families such as the Dunlops, Tennants, Magills, Camerons, etc., are to this day (1879) leaders of the tobacco trade of Petersburg, which has grown so great as to swallow up her sisters, Blandford and Pocahontas, which were merged in one corporation in 1784." David Hunter McAlpin (b. 1816) was one of the largest tobacco manufacturers; and Alexander Cameron, born in 1834 at Grantown-on-Spey, had an extensive share in the tobacco business, with four large branch factories in Australia. Alexander Macdonald (b. 1833), born at Forres, Elginshire, was President of the Standard Oil Company of Kentucky and Director in several other important business enterprises. James Crow, Kentucky pioneer, (c. 1800-1859), born in Scotland and graduated as a physician from Edinburgh University. In 1822 went from Philadelphia to Woodford County, Kentucky, where his knowledge of chemistry enabled him vastly to improve the methods of distilling whisky, and he became the founder of the great distilling industry of that state. Walter Callender, born in Stirling in 1834, was founder of the firm of Callender, McAuslan, and Troup, of Providence. E. J. Lindsay, born in Dundee in 1838, was manufacturer of agricultural implements in Wisconsin. Alexander Cochrane, born at Barrhead in 1840, was a great chemical manufacturer. Edwin Allen Cruikshank, born in 1843 of Scottish ancestry, was a real estate operator and one of the founders of the Real Estate Exchange in 1883. George Harrison Barbour, born in 1843 of Scottish parentage, was Vice-President and General Manager of the Michigan Stove Company, the largest establishment of the kind in the world. William Marshall, born in Leith in 1848, was founder of the Anglo-American Varnish Company (1890). Robert Means Thompson, born in 1849 of Scottish ancestry, was President of the Orford Copper Company, one of the largest producers of nickel in the world. William James Hogg (b. 1851), carpet manufacturer in Worcester and Auburn, Massachusetts; and Francis Thomas Fletcher Lovejoy, Secretary of the Carnegie Steel Company were of Scottish descent. William Howe McElwain (b. 1867), shoe manufacturer in New England, is of Argyllshire descent; and the Armours of Chicago, descended from James Armour, who came from Ulster c. 1750, claim

Scottish ancestry. William Barbour (b. 1847), thread manufacturer, was grandson of a Scot who moved from Paisley, Scotland, to Lisburn, Ireland, in 1768, and in 1784 established what is now the oldest linen thread manufacturing establishment in the world. George A. Clark (1824-73), born in Paisley, established the thread mills at Newark, New Jersey, the business of which was carried on by his brother William (b. 1841), who came to the United States in 1860. The great Coates Thread Mills at Pawtucket, Rhode Island, are a branch of the firm of J. and J. Coates of Paisley. Hugh Chalmers (b. 1873), President of the Chalmers Motor Company, of Detroit, is descended from Thomas Chalmers who came from Scotland early in the nineteenth century. Ramsey Crooks (1786-1859), fur trader, born in Greenock, Scotland; came to America and settled in Wisconsin. In 1809, he entered the service of John Jacob Astor and made, with Donald Mackenzie and Robert Stuart, the memorable 3,500-mile trip to Astoria, on the Pacific Ocean. In 1834, he settled in New York and engaged successfully in business. During his residence at Mackinac Island, Mich., and on his adventurous trips he was a great friend and confidant of the Indians. Black Hawk said he was "The best paleface friend the red men ever had. Mention may also here be made of the Anchor line of Steamships founded by Thomas and John Henderson of Glasgow. The ships of this line began service between Glasgow and New York in 1856. In 1869 they established a North Sea service between Granton, Scotland, and Scandinavian ports and through this channel introduced many thousands of industrious Scandinavian settlers into the United States. In 1870 they established the first direct communication between Italy, southern Europe and the United States, and in 1873 they inaugurated, and were the principal carriers of, the live cattle trade between the United States and Europe.

SCOTS IN BANKING, FINANCE, INSURANCE AND RAILROADS

In the financial and commercial field in this country the Scots have held a foremost place and stand unrivalled for integrity, energy, fidelity, and enterprise. Many jibes are made at the expense of the Canny Scot, but American business men have realized his value. In business and commercial life the success of the average Scot is remarkable and many of the guiding spirits among America's successful business men are Scots or men of Scottish descent.

James Blair (b. 1807), brother of John Inslee Blair, was largely identified with the development of banks and railroads in Pennsylvania. George Smith (1808-99), born in Aberdeenshire, founded the Wisconsin Marine and Fire Insurance Company (1839) and was later a prominent banker in Georgia. Alexander Mitchell (1817-87), financier, railroad builder, and one of the Commissioners of Public Debt of Milwaukee, was born near Ellon, Aberdeenshire. Brown Brothers, bankers in New York, was founded by Alexander Brown (1764-1834) who was born in Ballymena of Ulster Scot parentage. George Bain (1836-91), merchant, banker, and director in many railroads, banks, and insurance companies, was born in Stirling, Scotland. Robert Craig Chambers (b. 1831), miner, financier, and State Senator of Utah, was of Scottish descent. John Aikman Stewart (b. 1822), President of the United States Trust Company and Assistant Treasurer of the United States, was born in New York city, son of a native of Stornoway, Hebrides. Alonzo Barton Hepburn (b. 1847), descendant of Patrick Hepburn who came from Scotland in 1736, President of the Chase National Bank, a distinguished New York banker, has written much on financial subjects. Thomas William Lamont (b. 1870), whose forefather came from Argyllshire, is a member of the firm of J. P. Morgan & Co., and prominent in international finance. Walter Edwin Frew, President of the Corn Exchange Bank, New York, and President of the New York Clearing House is of Scottish parentage. He was a pioneer of the branch banking system in New York. James Berwick Forgan, born in St. Andrews, in 1852, President of the First National Bank of Chicago, is a pillar of finance. Andrew Glassell (1827-1901), descendant of a Dumfriesshire emigrant of 1756, was a prominent lawyer and banker in Los Angeles James Alexander Linen (b. 1840), President of the First National Bank of Scranton, was of Scottish parentage. George Rutledge Gibson (b. 1853), of Scottish descent, has written largely on questions of foreign finance. John Hall McClement (b. 1862), railroad and financial expert, is of Scottish parentage. Duncan MacInnes, born at Inveresk, near Edinburgh, has been Chief Accountant of the City of New York for many years, and is one of the best equipped men in municipal finance in America. Robert Graham Dun (1826-1900), mercantile credit expert, was grandson of Rev. James Dun, minister in Glasgow, who emigrated to Virginia, c. 1815.

Robert Burns Beath (1839-1914), President of the United Firemens' Insurance Company of Philadelphia, and author of the "History of the Grand Army of the Republic" (1888), was of Scots parentage. William C. Alexander (1806-74), President of the Equitable Life Insurance Company, was second son of Dr. Archibald Alexander of Princeton. His son James Waddell Alexander (1839-1915), was also President of the same Company. John Augustine McCall (1849-1906), President of the New York Life Insurance Company, was of Ulster Scot descent.

Men of Scottish birth or Scottish descent have had a prominent place in the development of the railroads of the United States from their inception to the present day. It was a Scot, Peter Fleming, Surveyor of the upper part of New York city, who laid out the grades for the first railroad in the state. John Inslee (or Insley) Blair (1802-99), founder of the Lackawanna Coal and Iron Company (1846), financier and founder of the Delaware and Lackawanna Railroad, was a descendant of Samuel Blair who came from Scotland in 1720. Blairstown, New Jersey, is named in his honor. He gave half a million dollars to various Presbyterian institutions. Samuel Sloan (1817-1907), President of the Delaware and Lackawanna Railroad (1867-99), was born in Lisburn of Ulster Scot ancestry. John T. Grant (1813-87), railroad builder in Georgia, Alabama, Tennessee, Mississippi, Louisiana, and Texas, was of Scottish origin; and so also was Thomas Alexander Scott (1824-81), Vice-President and President of the Pennsylvania Railroad, Assistant Secretary of War (1861-62), and President of the Texas Pacific Railroad. James McCrea (b. 1836), descended from James McCrea, an Ulster Scot who came to America in 1776, was one of the ablest Presidents of the Pennsylvania Railroad. John Edgar Thompson, third President, Frank Thompson, sixth Vice-President of the Pennsylvania system, were also of Scottish descent. Alexander Johnson Cassatt, seventh President, was

Scottish on his mother's side. Another prominent Scot connected
with the Pennsylvania Railroad was Robert Pitcairn, born at Johnstone, near Paisley, in 1836. Angus Archibald McLeod (b.
1847), re-organizer of the Philadelphia and Reading Raliroad was also a
Scot; and George Devereux Mackay (b. 1854), banker and railroad
builders, was descended from John Mackay who came from Caithness
in 1760. John Allan Muir (1852-1904), railroad promoter of California, was of Scottish parentage.

SCOTS AS JOURNALISTS, PUBLISHERS AND TYPEFOUNDERS

The first newspaper printed in North America, *The Boston News-Letter* for April 24, 1704, was published by a Scot, John Campbell (1653-1728), bookseller and postmaster of Bòston. John Mein and John Fleming, the founders and publishers of *The Boston Chronicle* (1767) were both born in Scotland. The paper was printed "on a new and handsome type, a broad faced long primer, from an Edinburgh foundry, and typographically far surpassed any paper that had appeared before it in New England." David Hall (c. 1714-1772), born in Edinburgh, emigrated to America shortly after 1740, became a partner of Benjamin Franklin in 1748. He was printer of the *Pennsylvania Gazette,* one of the few leading newspapers of the day, and one of the founders of the St. Andrew's Society of Philadelphia. His son, William (died 1831), who carried on the printing business, was one of the original members of the "Light Horse of the City of Philadelphia," afterwards known as "The First City Troop," and served in the Continental Army during the Revolutionary War. Robert Aitken (1734-1802), born in Dalkeith, Scotland, printer and publisher in Philadelphia in 1769, was publisher of the *Pennsylvania Magazine* from January 1775 to June 1776, the first magazine in Philadelphia containing illustrations, most of which were engraved by Aitken himself. He also published, at his own expense, in 1782, the first English Bible printed in America. Major Andrew Brown (c. 1744-1797), born in the north of Ireland of Scottish parents, was publisher of the *Federal Gazette,* later (1793) changed to *Philadelphia Gazette.* He is credited with being the first newspaper man to employ a reporter for the debates in Congress. It may here be mentioned that the publisher of the first directory of Philadelphia and its suburbs (1782), was a Scot, Captain John Macpherson (1726-92). James Adams, Delaware's first printer (1761), was an Ulster Scot who learned the art of printing in Londonderry and founded the *Wilmington Courant* in 1762. Col. Eleazer Oswald (1755-1795), of Scottish origin, though born in England, rendered brilliant service on the side of the colonies during the Revolution. In 1779 he became associated with William Goddard in the *Maryland Journal,* the first newspaper printed in Baltimore. Later removing to Philadelphia he issued the first number of the *Independent Gazetteer, or the Chronicle of Freedom,* April 13, 1782, and at th same time he also conducted in New York *The Independent Gazetteer, or New York Journal* (1782-87). The first daily paper published in Baltimore (1791) was by David Graham. Alexander Purdie, a native of Scotland, was editor of the *Virginia Gazette* from March 1766 to December 1774. Shortly after this date he started a Gazette of his own, and in the issue of his paper for June 7, 1776, he printed the heraldic device of a shield, on which is a rattlesnake coiled, with supporters, dexter, a bear collared and chained, sinister, a stag. The crest is a woman's head crowned and the motto: *Don't tread on me.* Adam Boyd (1738-1803), colonial printer and preacher, purchased the printing outfit of another Scot, Andrew Stuart, who had set up the first printing press in Wilmington, North Carolina, in 1763. In 1769 (Oct. 13) Boyd issued the first number of the *Cape Fear Mercury,* and continued it till 1776. James Johnston, born in Scotland, was the first to establish a printing press in Georgia (1762) and in April, 1763, began publication of *The Georgia Gazette,* which was published by him for twenty-seven years. His successor (1793) was another Scot, Alexander M'Millan, "Printer to the State." Robert Wells (1728-94), born in Scotland, was a publisher and bookseller in South Carolina for many years, and published the *South Carolina and American General Gazette.* John Wells, Florida's first printer (1784), born in Charleston, served his apprenticeship at Donaldson's printing house in Edinburgh. Matthew Duncan, son of Major Joseph Duncan, of Scottish ancestry, introduced printing into Illinois in 1809, and published the first newspaper there. Major Nathaniel McLean, brother of John McLean, one of the Justices of the Supreme Court of the United States, was one of the first publishers in Minnesota (1849, the same year in which printing was introduced into the state). The township of McLean, Ramsey county, was named in honor of him. There is mention of a printing press being set up in Michigan in 1785 by Alexander and William Macomb, but nothing further is known of it. The first book printed in Montana was in 1864, and in August of the same year John Buchanan founded the *Montana Post at* Virginia City. John Dunlap (1747-1812), an Ulster Scot born in Strabane, was Congressional Printer and first printed the Declaration of Independence.

Thomas Ritchie (1778-1854), born of Scottish parentage. He wielded a powerful influence for good in both the national and state politics of Virginia, and his funeral was attended by nearly all the distinguished men of the times, including the President. Ritchie County, West Virginia, was named in his honor. Francis Preston

Blair (1791-1876), political writer, negotiator of peace conference at Hampton Roads in 1864, and editor of the Washington *Globe*, was a descendant of Commissary Blair of Virginia. James Gordon Bennett (1795-1872), born near Keith, Banffshire, pioneer of modern American journalism and founder of the New York *Herald*, a newspaper which has long wielded a great influence on political affairs. Horace Greeley (1811-72), founder of the New York *Tribune*, unsuccessful candidate for the Presidency in 1872, anti-slavery leader, and author of "The American Conflict" (1864-66), was of Ulster Scot descent. Of the same origin was Joseph Medill (1823-99), proprietor of the Chicago *Tribune* (1874); and Robert Bonner (1824-99), founder of the New York *Ledger* (1851), was born in Londonderry of Ulster Scot origin. James Thompson Callender (d. 1806), a political exile from Scotland, a controversial writer of great power, a severe critic of the administration of John Adams, founded the *Richmond Recorder*, predecessor of the *Richmond Enquirer*. John Swinton (1829-1901), born in Haddingtonshire, was editorial writer for the New York *Times* (1860-70), and *Sun* (1875-83, 1893-97). He took an active interest in social and industrial questions and was Progressive Labor Party's candidate for State Senator in 1887. James Redpath (1833-91), journalist and author, born in Berwick-on-Tweed, was prominently identified with the abolition movement, was organizer of the school system of South Carolina, founder of the Boston Lyceum Bureau, war correspondent for Northern newspapers during the Civil War, and author of several histories and biographical works. William Andrew Ure (b. 1839), of Scottish parentage, by his energy made the Newark, New Jersey, *Sunday Call*, one of the leading newspapers in the state. Whitelaw Reid is noted under Ambassadors. St. Clair McKelway (b. 1845), who became Regent and Vice-Chancellor of the University of the State of New York, was of Scots parentage. Andrew McLean, born in 'Renton, Dumbartonshire, in 1848, is editor-in-chief of the *Brooklyn Citizen*, which under his guidance has become an influential paper. Washington McLean and his son, John R. McLean, established one of the greatest newspapers in the Middle West, the *Cincinnati Enquirer*. David Alexander Munro (1848-1910), a native of Maryburgh, Ross-shire, educated at Edinburgh University, editor for many years of the *North American Review*. John Foord, born in Perthshire, came to the U. S. in 1869; became editorial writer on the *New York Times* and later editor-in-chief; after 1883, editor and publisher of the *Brooklyn Union;* editor of *Harper's Weekly;* leader writer on *Journal of Commerce,* and editor of *Asia.* Other journalists who may be mentioned are William Cauldwell (b. 1824) of New York, of Scottish parentage on both sides; George Dawson

(1813-83) of Albany, born in Falkirk, Scotland; William Wiston Seaton (1785-1866) of Washington, D. C., a Regent of the Smithsonian Institution; and George Horace Lorimer (b. 1867), journalist and author of "Letters from a Self-made Merchant to His Son" (1902), etc. John J. McElhone (1832-90), famous as a stenographer and chief Official Reporter of the House of Representatives, was of Scotish ancestry.

Thomas Dobson, publisher of the first American edition of the Encyclopaedia Britannica (1791), was a Scot who gave a great impulse to printing in the United States. Robert Carter (1807-89), publisher and founder of the house of Robert Carter and Brothers, so long and honorably known in New York city, was born in Earlston, Berwickshire. Henry Ivison (1808-84), born in Glasgow, became a prominent publisher in New York. His son, David Brinkerhoff Ivison, born in 1835, was also a prominent publisher and founder of the American Book Company. John Wilson (1802-68), born in Glasgow, was founder of the famous printing firm of John Wilson and Son of Cambridge, Massachusetts, now Harvard University Press. George Munro (1825-96), publisher of the Seaside Library, Fireside Companion, etc., was of Scottish descent. In the course of his life he gave away half a million dollars for educational purposes. Whatever may be thought of his appropriating the works of British authors without compensation it cannot be denied that he did a great deal to raise the literary taste among the poorer classes in this country. George William Childs (1829-94), publisher and proprietor of the Philadelphia Public Ledger, was of Scottish descent. Robert Clarke (1829-99), founded of the great Cincinnati publishing house of Robert Clarke and Co., was born in the town of Annan in Dumfriesshire. Norman Leslie Munro (1842-94), publisher of the Family Story Paper and founder of Munro's Publishing House, was born in Nova Scotia of Scottish ancestry.

John Baine, born in St. Andrews, in partnership with his grandson, established the first type-foundry in Philadelphia in 1787. Their firm cast the types for a portion of the American edition of the Encyclopaedia Britannica, reprinted in Philadelphia in 1791. Archibald Binny, (1763-1838), born in Portobello, near Edinburgh, and James Ronaldson (d. 1841), also born in Scotland, succeeded to and carried on the business established by Baine. In 1797 they cast the first $ sign used in this country. The quality and art of their product was in no wise inferior to the European and the sale of foreign made types ceased shortly after they established their business. Their foundry kept pace with the growth of the country and in the seventies of last century became the best and most extensive letter-foundry in the world. Archibald Binny loaned the United States Government the sum of 50,000 dollars for use in the war of 1812-14. Ronaldson was first president of the Franklin Institute in Philadelphia (1824-41), an institution in which he took a great interest, and in 1831 presented to Philadelphia the beautiful cemetery bearing his name. He was described as "an upright, frugal and honest man, and a lover of his adopted country." George Bruce (1781-1866), born in Edinburgh, along with his brother David introduced the art of stereotyping, the secret of which David secured in Edinburgh. In 1816 they purchased a foundry for type making and stereotyping, and George Bruce in his seventy-eighth year of age produced type which has rarely been excelled for beauty of design and neatness of finish. "He did much toward facilitating American printing and towards making it a fine art, inventing; with the assistance of his nephew, David Bruce, Jr., a successful type-casting machine which has come into general use." Thomas Mackellar (1812-1899), printer and poet, also one of the leading type founders, was of Scottish parentage. William Vincent McKean, born in 1820 of Ulster Scot descent, was another distinguished type-founder and editor-in-chief of the *Philadelphia Public Ledger* for many years. Another individual who may be included under this head is Adam Ramage who was born in Scotland and died at an advanced age in Philadelphia in 1850. He was distinguished as a manufacturer of printing presses in the beginning of last century, and patented the "Ramage" press in 1818.

SOME PROMINENT SCOTS IN NEW YORK CITY

Many names mentioned in other sections apply equally to New York city but for lack of space they are not here again referred to. David Jamison, one of the early Colonial lawyers in New York, was born in Scotland. In 1707 he defended Francis Makemie, the Presbyterian clergyman, when he was arrested for preaching in the city without a license, and in 1710 he became Chief Justice of New Jersey. James Graham (died c. 1700), Recorder of the city, was also a native of Scotland. John Watts (1749-1836), of Scots parentage, was the last Royal Recorder of the city, Speaker of the New York Assembly, Member of Congress, 1793-96, and founder of the Leake and Watts Orphan Asylum. Archibald Gracie, born in Dumfries, emigrated to America about 1778. Through his business enterprise he largely developed the commercial importance of the port of New York. He was also founder of the first Savings Bank in America, founder of the Lying-In Hospital of the Cedar Street Presbyterian Church, President of the Chamber of Commerce for twenty years, etc. Cadwallader David Colden (1769-1834), grandson of Cadwallader Colden, was Mayor of the city from 1818 to 1821, and made an enviable record in that office. James Lenox (1800-80), merchant, philanthropist, bibliophile, and founder of the Lenox Library, now incorporated in the New York Public Library, was one of the most useful citizens New York ever possessed. His public benefactions were numerous, but only the largest were made public. Among these were the Lenox Library, formerly at Fifth Avenue and Seventieth Street; the Presbyterian Hospital, and liberal endowments to Princeton University and Princeton Theological Seminary. Alexander Turney Stewart (1803-76), merchant and philanthropist, born in Ireland of Scots parents, established the great dry goods business now owned by John Wanamaker. He was nominated as Secretary of the Treasury (1869) but was not confirmed. Hugh Maxwell (1787-1873), born in Paisley, was Assistant Junior Advocate General in 1814, District Attorney for the city from 1819 to 1829, and Collector of the Port (1849-52). Robert L. Stuart (1806-82) and his brother Alexander (1810-79), sugar refiners, both gave large sums, estimated at over two million dollars, to many charities, and the library, pictures, and mineral and shell collections of the former are preserved in a separate room of the New York Public Library.   Hugh Auchincloss (1817-90) and John Auchincloss, his brother, sons of Hugh Auchincloss of Paisley, were prominent merchants in the city.   Robert Lenox Kennedy (b. 1822), banker and public spirited citizen, grandson of a Scot, was President of the Trustees of the New York Public Library, an institution largely Scottish in its foundation and endowment.   James Gibb, born in Scotland in 1829, a successful merchant, was President of Brooklyn Park Commission.   James Cruikshank (b. 1831), of Scottish descent, was noted for his activity in furthering education in Brooklyn.   Abram Stevens Hewitt (1822-1903), of Scottish parentage, was Member of Congress from New York (1875-79, 1881-86), and Mayor of the city (1887-88).   John Stewart Kennedy (1830-1909), financier and philanthropist, born at Blantyre, near Glasgow, gave one million dollars to the Presbyterian Hospital as his golden wedding anniversary gift, five hundred thousand dollars to Columbia University, besides innumerable gifts to other institutions.   His will left over sixty-seven million dollars, nearly half of it for charitable purposes.   Alexander Ector Orr (1831-1914), President of New York Rapid Transit Commission, Vice-President of many financial institutions, was of Ulster Scot descent.   Thomas Fitchie (1834-1905), of Scottish parentage, was an earnest worker for purity in civil life in Brooklyn.   Charles A. Lamont (1835-1904), son of Neil Lamont from Scotland, was one of the original members of the Republican Party and of the Union League prominent in city affairs.   He was the originator of the Ramapo scheme of water supply for the city.   Robert Maclay (b. 1836), of Scottish parentage, was President of the Knickerbocker Ice Company (1875), Commissioner of Education, Rapid Transit Commissioner, etc.   Dr. Albert Prescott Marble (1836-1906), a recognized leader in educational matters, President of the Board of Superintendents of the New York Department of Education, was a descendant of one of the Scots settlers of Maine.   Robert Macy Galloway (b. 1837), merchant and banker, had a considerable part in developing the elevated railroads of the city.   Eugene Gilbert Blackford (1839-1904), merchant and ichthyologist, of Scottish descent, "did more to advance the interests of fish culture in this country than any other man."   He wrote much on the subject and to his efforts was due the creation of the Aquarium at the Battery.   Alexander Taylor, born in Leith, Scotland, in 1821, was founder of the firm of Alexander Taylor's Sons.   Walter Scott, managing Director of Butler Brothers, born in Canada, of Scottish parentage, is widely known as a liberal promoter of education, art, athletics, and patriotism.

SCOTTISH SOCIETIES IN THE UNITED STATES

That the Scots in America have not been solely devoted to business and the promotion of their own selfish welfare is evidenced by the remarkable growth of their numerous Societies based upon the extension of fellowship among Scots in the New World and for the collection and distribution of charitable funds among the poor and needy of their countrymen. The oldest of these Societies, the Scots' Charitable Society of Boston, was founded January 6, 1657, with twenty-seven members. It was followed by the St. Andrew's Club of Charleston, S. C. (the first to bear the name of St. Andrew), 1729; the St. Andrew's Society of Philadelphia, December 7, 1749; the St. Andrew's Society of Savannah, Ga., 1750; the St. Andrew's Society of the Province, afterward of the State of New York, November 19, 1756; and the St. Andrew's Society of Albany, N. Y., November 10, 1803; until at the present time, there is no city of any size or importance in the country that does not have its St. Andrew's Society, or Burns or Caledonian Club, which serves to keep alive the memories of the home-land, to instil patriotism toward the adopted country, and to aid the distressed among their kinsfolk. There are now more than one thousand of these Societies in America, including the Order of Scottish Clans (organized, 1878) a successful fraternal, patriotic and beneficial order, with more than one hundred separate clans, and the Daughters of Scotia, a rapidly growing order for women of Scottish blood, organized in 1898.

CONCLUSION

"It is the knowledge that Scotsmen have done their share in building up the great Republic that makes them proud of its progress and inspires them to add to its glories and advantages in every way. Scotsmen, as a nationality, are everywhere spoken of as good and loyal citizens, while Americans who can trace a family residence of a century in the country are proud if they can count among their ancestors some one who hailed from the land of Burns, and it is a knowledge of all this, in turn, that makes the American Scot of to-day proud of his country's record and his citizenship and impels him to be as devoted to the new land as it was possible for him to have been to the old had he remanied in it. In America, the old traditions, the old blue flag with its white cross, the old Doric, are not forgotten, but are nourished, and preserved, and honored, and spoken by Scotsmen on every side with the kindliest sentiments on the part of those to whom they are alien. Americans know and acknowledge that the traditions and flag and homely speech have long been conserved to the development of that civil and religious liberty on which the great confederation of sovereign republican States has been founded. In the United States, Sir Walter Scott has more readers and quite as enthusiastic admirers as in Scotland, and if Americans were asked which of the world's poets came nearest to their hearts, the answer would undoubtedly be—Robert Burns."

LIST OF PRINCIPAL AUTHORITIES REFERRED TO

Appleton. Cyclopædia of American Biography. New York, 1887-89. 6v.

Bingham. Early History of Michigan. Lansing, 1888.

Breed. Presbyterians and the Revolution. Philadelphia, 1876.

Campbell. The Puritan in Holland, England, and America. New York, 1892.

Casson. The Sons of Old Scotland in America. New York, 1906.

Charlton. The Making of Georgia. Savannah, 1905.

Craighead. Scotch and Irish Seeds in American Soil. Philadelphia, 1879.

Dinsmore. The Scotch-Irish in America. Chicago, 1906.

Dyer. Early American Craftsmen. New York, 1915.

Ford. The Scotch-Irish in America. Princeton, 1915.

Green. The Scotch-Irish in America. Worcester, 1895.

Hanna. The Scotch-Irish. New York, 1902. 2 v.

Harrison. The Scot in Ulster. Edinburgh, 1888.

Jones. History of Georgia. Boston, 1883.

Kelly and Burrage. American Medical Biographies. Baltimore, 1920.

Lewis. Great American Lawyers. Philadelphia, 1907-09. 8 v.

Maclean. Historical Account of the Settlements of Scottish Highlanders in America Prior to the Peace of 1783. Cleveland, 1900.

National Cyclopædia of American Biography. New York, 1898-1906. 16 v.

Parker. History of Londonderry, New Hampshire. Boston, 1851.

Register of the Privy Council of Scotland. Edinburgh, v. 8, 9.

Reid. The Scot in America and the Ulster Scot. London, 1911.

Roberts. New York-Boston, 1904.

Ross. The Scot in America. New York, 1896.

Scotch-Irish in America. Proceeding of Scotch-Irish Congresses.

Scots Magazine. Edinburgh, 1768-1774.

Slaughter. History of Bristol Parish. Richmond, 1879.

Smith. History of the Colony of Nova Cæsaria or New Jersey. Burlington, 1765.

Smith. History of New York. Philadelphia, 1792.

White. Southern Presbyterian Leaders. New York, 1911.

INDEX

Date Due